Touey & Lucey Publishing

Philadelphia, Pennsylvania

2018

ISBN: 978-0-692-97294-6

Printed in United States of America

Library of Congress Control Number: 2018946429

Cover photo by Melvin Epps thirdeyepro.com

Cover design by Mary Ann Smith

For more information:

Sr. Jeannette Lucey, IHM

3040 Cottman Ave. Philadelphia, PA 19149

Email: jlucey1105@gmail.com

To Order More Copies, go to TheWelcomeSchool.com

TABLE OF CONTENTS

DEDICATION

This book is dedicated to the many children who fled their native lands and who, as immigrants and refugees, made their way with their families to St. Francis de Sales School in West Philadelphia during our many years there—and to the predominantly African American children who welcomed them.

Sisters Constance and Jeannette

March 25, 2018

ACKNOWLEDGMENTS

Writing a book for the first time is a monumental undertaking, and we owe our thanks to those who shared their knowledge and expertise with us. Initially, we wrote the stories of our children.

- Next, Terry McNally rearranged, revised, redrafted and improved the tales and probed us with questions that expanded our horizons.

- Then, we met Michael Brown and Kathleen Labonge who used their exceptional skills to check every detail and edit the manuscript.

- Finally, Mary Ann Smith formatted the book and created the delightful cover.

- Alan Schiff reviewed the manuscript, posed critical questions and offered his enduring support to this project.

- However, Judy Stavisky, our advisor, guide, and longtime friend was the driving force who kept us going during discouraging times. Judy also tracked down all the alums in the "Grads Look Back" sections and conducted phone and personal interviews so they could appear in the book.

Finally, we thank our IHM Community who assigned us to our life-changing ministry at St. Francis de Sales School and supported this project. AMEN!

INTRODUCTION

Do <u>you</u> believe in kids—in their innate abilities and indomitable spirits?

<u>We</u> do! And that's why we wrote this book.

The two of us met in 1984 and have worked together just about every day since. Year after year, immigration wave after immigration wave, we watched boys and girls enter St. Francis de Sales School in West Philadelphia, overcome daunting challenges, and end up exceeding everyone's expectations—everyone's, that is, except ours.

"How did they do it?" People aware of our students' success often asked us that question. To answer it, we told stories about the students and some of their life experiences. Some of the tales drew laughter, some tears, but inevitably the listener's final response was, "You two should write a book!"

And so, we did. In the beginning, the book was to be about the children, and <u>only</u> the children. Then our colleague, Terry McNally, shared the manuscript with five professional writers in California. He told us that all five of them asked, "Who are these two nuns?" Terry then guided us through introducing ourselves. This story is about our early years at de Sales, mostly the first 10 of 31 years. It all happened with the tireless energy and dedication so many of our Sisters and lay teachers exhibited in each of those classrooms and <u>before</u> we met the cherished friends, graduates, and benefactors who were responsible for the growth and expansion of the school and so many innovative programs. To begin to name the hundreds of teachers, friends, grads, and benefactors for so many years, we would run the risk of neglecting to name a few. Instead, we extend our love and gratitude to each of you!

Sisters Constance Marie Touey and Jeannette Lucey, IHM

March 25, 2018

(Please note: Sometimes the names of children have been changed to protect their identity, but each story is real and true as we remember it.)

CHAPTER ONE

We Had Nothing, Yet We Had Everything

The convent is just like the Army; you don't have a choice. You simply get a letter saying, "You are appointed by Holy Obedience to . . ." such and such.

---

†

J. M. J. A. T.
Villa Maria House of Studies
Immaculata, Pennsylvania 19345

Dear   Sister Mary Jeannette, I.H.M.

You are appointed by Holy Obedience

to: St. Francis de Sales

for: Grade 8

May God bless your obedience, dear Sister.

Devotedly, in Mary's Immaculate Heart,

Mother Marie Dominic   I.H.M.

Feast: Saint Anthony
June 13, 1984

In 1984, the two of us received letters assigning us to St. Francis de Sales School (SFDS) in distressed West Philadelphia—Sister Constance as principal, Sister Jeannette to teach eighth grade.

Despite being part of the same religious order, Sisters of the Immaculate Heart of Mary (IHM), we had never met.

Each of us came with more than two decades of experience in elementary education, but from very dissimilar types of schools. Sister Constance had been an elementary principal but never before worked in an urban school; Sister Jeannette, on the other hand, was a veteran of city schools.

OUR NEW HOME

The co-ed K–8 school, a four-story granite-block structure, was built in 1904. The Sisters who taught in the school lived in the convent across the street from the school. The church, an imposing piece of Byzantine Revival architecture with a huge tile dome, followed a few years later.

St. Francis de Sales School is on South 47ʰ Street, a few miles from the University of Pennsylvania. The Church is at the corner of Springfield Avenue and South 47ʰ Street.

As Philadelphia's hardworking Irish immigrants prospered, so did the parish. Its 4,000 families provided enormous spirit and financial support that gave the congregation and school a prominent place in the Philadelphia Archdiocese. Three pastors were Bishops, which was most unusual. The Boys Choir had a national reputation, and many school graduates became priests and nuns. Indeed, the school had served as a demonstration site where Sisters and lay teachers from all over the area came to observe new teaching methods and classroom procedures.

But all that began to change in the 1950s and 1960s as more and more Irish families moved to the suburbs, replaced by primarily non-Catholic African American families, leaving parish upkeep to an increasingly fewer number of parishioners. Eventually, this once-wealthy and generous parish—for years St. Francis supported new Catholic churches and schools in the suburbs—simply ran out of money and became dependent on contributions from the Archdiocesan office in downtown Philadelphia. The parish was "on the dole."

A DIFFICULT BEGINNING

That was the state of affairs when we arrived, and the school very much reflected it. Moss, nurtured by leaking bathroom pipes, sprouted from the granite exterior, and the school yard was blanketed by cracked cement. Inside, the classrooms needed paint, and the auditorium floor was spotted with metal patches to cover holes worn in the wood below. And it was not just a matter of cosmetics. We were without a gym teacher, an art teacher, and a music teacher. Most critically, the school's enrollment had shrunk to 400 boys and girls from a high of 1,400 students.

Along with the church and school, the surrounding neighborhood had also fallen on hard times. Many of the once-handsome old Victorian houses were deteriorating and literally falling apart. Driving by one apartment building not far from the school, we saw mothers and children with pots and pans collecting water from a fire hydrant; they had no running water in their building, we later learned.

In short, our introduction to St. Francis was not an auspicious one.

Sister Jeannette:

I arrived at de Sales in early August and discovered that the new principal had not yet appeared. What's more, I learned that four teachers had resigned. I had just completed 15 years teaching in distressed areas of the city, and I knew how difficult it would be to find replacements. I remember saying to myself, "This is definitely not a good beginning. I'm really worried."

Sister Constance:

I was a few days late arriving because I had spent the summer working in a very poor area of Appalachia in Kentucky. I showed up with great confidence, eager to get started . . . until I found out that four teachers had quit. That first day I ran into Sister Jeannette in the convent kitchen. I saw that she was wearing her habit but had not yet put on her veil. She was about 5' 6" tall and thin, with thick, dark hair and bangs, blue eyes, and nun glasses—round and wire-rimmed. We chatted a bit, and in the course of our very first conversation, she announced, "I hate kids!"

I didn't know her well enough to respond but was ready to cry. Of course, as I learned later, she didn't hate kids at all; it was a joke—a running one. But at the time, I missed the humor. "Oh dear, isn't this a shame?" I was thinking, "The eighth grade is so important in kids' lives. To have a nun that hates kids is a tragedy!"

Sister Jeannette:

I had heard of Sister Constance in the community

but had never met her. She struck me as a textbook nun: slim, about 5'2" tall, beautiful blue eyes, light brown hair sticking out from under the veil, and a ready smile. My first impression was that she seemed laid back, almost phlegmatic—pleasant enough, but perhaps not quite ready for the job, particularly since she hadn't arrived in time to hire the teachers we needed.

The day after her arrival, Sister Constance interviewed her first prospective teacher. I was so anxious and hung around to hear the outcome. When the handsome, sharply dressed, hopeful young man left, I said, "What grade will he teach?" She responded, "Oh, I didn't hire him. I like to interview six or seven and then pick the best one."

It suddenly hit me: this nun has no clue! I all but screamed, "You'll never get that many applicants to come here. You've got to hire <u>him</u>!" And after failing for three days to get anyone else to even come for an interview, that's exactly what she did.

A frantic search for teachers consumed the next three weeks. We called all around for leads: Drexel, University of Pennsylvania, St. Joseph's, Temple. Just getting people to come into the neighborhood for an interview was a huge challenge. We could hear several fellows who accompanied female prospects mumbling, "I don't want my girlfriend working here."

The slots were finally filled, in part with family members; the new hires included two nephews of Sister Constance. The last recruit—for one of the school's two first grade classes—signed the day before school started. It was Sister Constance's first lesson at St. Francis: teachers were <u>not</u> banging on the doors to get into a school like this.

THE RICHEST OF BLESSINGS

But all of the negatives dissolved on opening day when the students lined up in the school yard. Standing amidst mostly African American and a few white youngsters were children from Vietnam, Thailand, Cambodia, and Laos who greeted us in their native languages. The group included part-time students from a nearby Catholic school for the visually impaired.

As we looked at these young faces, we knew we were seeing the true heart and soul of St. Francis de Sales. The school might be financially poor, but here was the richest of blessings. Despite our different teaching backgrounds and personalities, the two of us soon realized that we shared the same conviction: these students—many from communities hit hard by poverty and violence—could do anything if we believed in them.

We envision ourselves as missionaries. In our religious community we say that every place we are sent is "our mission." This school was definitely mission territory.

Sister Constance:

> *The sense that this was missionary work was very important. I would explain to every new lay teacher, "We are asking you to give your blood, sweat, and sometimes tears, and we will pay you peanuts. This is like the Peace Corps, but you get to go home every day." I wanted to be sure they knew what they were getting into.*

> *The new first-grade teacher—the one I hired the day before school started—couldn't leave her previous job in time to be on hand opening day. So I was the substitute. Teaching the children how to make the*

sign of the cross, I explained God's love for little children. "Jesus," I said, "loves you even more than your mother and father love you."

With that, a dark-skinned boy in the back of the room cried out, "But my mother doesn't love me. She left our family, and now we're all alone."

That was my second lesson: these children are in pain.

ABOUT THE TWO OF US

We both grew up in large Catholic families and went to schools taught by nuns of the Immaculate Heart of Mary (IHM) order, a community dedicated to education. We admired our teachers and wanted to be like them. That was why each of us decided to be a nun. But beyond that, our paths went in different directions—until they crossed at St. Francis de Sales.

Sister Constance:

> *I grew up in Lansdowne, a small town just outside of Philadelphia, the fifth of seven children in an Irish family. We were not well off. Dad sold insurance, and Mama worked as a secretary. I was the only one among my friends whose mother worked, and I missed seeing her when I got home from school. I remember it was my job every afternoon to start the potatoes.*
>
> *I knew I wanted to be a nun early on—by eighth grade—but I still enjoyed my friends very much and had an active social life. I loved to dance and sing, and still do. I did well in school, and for high school*

received a half-scholarship to a special Catholic academy.

But my mother felt that at the academy the gulf between the wealthier students and me would be too great, and we couldn't afford to make up the difference in tuition. So I stayed with my friends in the regular Catholic high school. It was a good decision, one with which I've always been happy.

I've taught every elementary grade level. I started off teaching for five years in a parish school in Drexel Hill in suburban Philadelphia and then spent six years in California in what is now called Silicon Valley. That was followed by a brief but wonderful stint back in Philadelphia in the city's Manayunk area and two years in the barriadas of Peru, where IHM nuns staff schools. Immediately prior to St. Francis de Sales, I spent 12 years in the Philadelphia suburb of West Chester, the last six as principal of St. Agnes Elementary.

I remember in my youth there was a song that began "Join the Navy and see the world." This small-town girl joined the convent and thought she had seen it all—until I got to St. Francis de Sales.

Sister Jeannette:

Easton, Pennsylvania, about 80 miles north of Philadelphia was my home, and I entered the convent at 17. Six weeks later—after intensive training by experienced IHM Sisters—I was teaching first grade in the blue-collar Philadelphia neighborhood of Frankford. That was 1959—in the days when classrooms were full and sisters were needed to staff them. I had 87 children squeezed together in my classroom that first year.

That's a lot of students, but I was the second oldest of 13 children, and anyone who grows up in a family that size knows how to maneuver and operate in a classroom. At home we sorted out the clothes by initials, so regimentation was familiar to me; the classroom was an extension of that experience.

I had also been a Girl Scout and a camp counselor, and teaching was more of the same. And I had so much energy in those days. I had been a cheerleader in high school, and sometimes in the evening another young sister (Beth) and I would go out in the backyard of the convent and do cheers, just for fun. Growing up, we often had silent meals at home—no talking until our plates were clean. So, it was nothing strange when we had silent meals at the convent. You learned to be contemplative.

After Frankford, I spent 10 years teaching in the Philadelphia suburbs. But I then came back to the city and remained there, teaching eighth grade for forty years. I taught a lot of kids who were hungry and went home to apartments without heat or water.

To believe in these kids—when so many others did not—became a personal crusade. I wanted to prove people wrong, to make them look at these kids through different lenses, and to celebrate and rejoice in all that these youngsters had to offer.

A GRADUATE LOOKS BACK:

Ameer Jones '02

Ameer Jones, 27, has a BS in mechanical engineering from Villanova University, and an MBA from the University of Florida. He works for Lockheed Martin and lives in Florida. He is married to Tashae Croxton, who also went to St. Francis de Sales. She is a Temple University graduate who also works at Lockheed Martin.

———

I started in a Philly public school. I was always a little advanced academically, and my father pulled me out so I would be more challenged. My dad and his 12 brothers and sisters all attended de Sales. In fact, my Nanna—my father's mom—used to teach there. Right from the beginning, I realized it had a lot more structure. Just having to wear a bright yellow shirt and blue tie had me thinking, "Man, they are strict here!" As I got older, I realized they weren't so much strict as structured.

That structure was what I needed coming up, and it was night and day compared to my public school. A lot of my friends in the neighborhood stayed in public school, and I always seemed to be two grades above them in what I was learning.

At first, it was different seeing nuns, but you got used to that after a while. Sister Constance, who knew my Nanna well, embraced me and made sure I had a smooth transition. Sister Jeannette did a lot of things that were unconventional. If you weren't paying attention, she would throw erasers at you. To this day, Sister J is still my favorite teacher. I loved her.

Sister J and Sister C always used to push me. When I spoke with them recently, they reminded me that when I first got there, I told them I wanted to do something to make my dad proud. I was a math geek and ended up good at "Math 24" and also won the highest general average medal at eighth grade graduation. I made my father proud!

SFDS was very diverse. There were students from Vietnam, China, Eritrea, Ethiopia, Ghana, Kenya, and other countries. So many different cultures exposed me to different ways of thinking at an early age, and I know I benefited. Going to school with students from all over the world has a huge effect on team dynamics. You don't fall into "group-think." On special days, kids told where they were from and shared a food dish related to their culture. Hearing my classmates talk about where they came from was eye opening, and the food was amazing. I remember one dish—chess pie brought by a girl from Kentucky. That pie was pretty good!

In fourth grade, I got into a fight after school. I don't remember what it was about, but I do remember Sister C was so upset with me. She told me I had broken her heart, and I felt terrible. She was tough on me and threatened to kick me out of school if I didn't turn things around. I wrote her a note later, "I am sorry your heart is in pieces. I promise you, I will never do that again." And I never did.

That was a turning point for me. I knew I was smart, but I realized then that I needed to act right too—to be a model student both in the books and outside the books.

For me, the most important lesson—during my time at de Sales but also afterwards—was the Sisters' perseverance. The school went through hard times, but the Sisters persevered. I admire them for that. They are fighters. I remember we had a faculty/student basketball game, and Sister C played every year. We had a special line for her to shoot foul shots from—a little closer to the basket; we called it the "Sister Constance" line. She would try so hard, and 95 percent of the time she made the free throws. You could see the competitive fire in her. And when she missed, she would get mad at herself. She wanted to win!

My father's been in prison since I was one year old, and he's fighting for his life right now on death row. Dad could have easily given up on his responsibilities, considering his situation. But he always made certain that he was a part of my life, and that is why I respect him so much. He was always there for me.

My three best friends are my mom, my dad, and my wife. I'm in Florida, but I talk to my dad more than I talk to anyone— four times a week: Tuesday night at 7, Thursday night at 7, and on the weekends. I give my mom a lot of credit, too. She felt it was important that we have a relationship with my dad and always took us to visit him.

Most of the men on my mom's side of the family have been in jail or have passed away. A neighbor once asked me, "How were you different from the rest of the men in your family?

What made it work for you?" I thought about this a lot. First, I think a lot of it is due to my parents. I feel blessed to have the parents that I have. Second, it's the neighborhood you grow up in and the company you keep. Most of my friends were at SFDS. We were all like-minded. And even my friends who did not go to SFDS didn't get into negative things. Third, education can be critical. In the communities that we come from, a lot of people don't value education. I was blessed that even when I was young, my mom and dad preached education to me. Mom would not let me go outside and play until I finished my homework. A lot of smart and ambitious kids went to SFDS. I was very competitive and wanted to be the smartest one in the group. I had to work and strive to achieve that.

SFDS holds a special place in my heart. I not only met some of my best friends there, but my wife attended as well. Her family moved away when she was in the sixth grade, but we later reconnected through a mutual friend.

CHAPTER TWO

The Gift We Offer Is Welcome

Upon our arrival at the school, we sensed a pervasive feeling of depression. The sisters and lay teachers were doing their best, but they were weary. Resignation was everywhere. So many had lowered their expectations of what was possible. There was no school Christmas play, not even Christmas singing. Anytime we asked what you do for this holiday or that feast day, the answer was always the same: "Well, we don't do anything."

In short, St. Francis seemed to be merely a place where children attended. Where was the excitement? The joy? That first year we showed a movie in the auditorium at Christmas time as a special treat. The kids walked in silently, their arms at their sides. The auditorium didn't have blackout curtains, and the sun was pouring in. In truth, you couldn't see a thing in the movie except that there was a dog, and occasionally its tail wagged. The children sat through the film without talking and left just as quietly.

ADDRESSING THE CHALLENGE

Part of the problem was a lack of resources. It's understandable that SFDS was without a computer in the school, but there wasn't even a copier—which we badly needed to put on a Christmas bazaar.

Sister Constance asked the pastor if he could give us the money to buy one. "Sister," he replied, "I don't have money for a copier." And he didn't.

Just keeping the school open took about $150,000 a year over and above what was collected in tuition. And parents struggled to pay even a modest tuition. That was a lot more money 35 years ago but not enough to pay for gym, art, and music teachers. The attitude of the Archdiocese, which provided the $150,000, was: "If we're supporting your school, then you make do with the minimum. Other schools need money, too."

One of the first things Sister Constance did was to apply for federal aid for low-income children under *Title I of the Elementary and Secondary Education Act*—part of Lyndon Johnson's War on Poverty. We received the funding that paid for a reading specialist and an ESOL teacher (English for Speakers of Other Languages).

Two trailers were provided by the federal government for improved student services. At that time, the feds would not allow Title One teachers to work inside a religious school, so one trailer was set up in the main school yard, the other next to the *Little School*—twin Victorian houses across the street that were converted years before into classrooms for the youngest children. Sister Constance also applied for and received a grant that funded the purchase of books and gym equipment.

Another problem was a sort of a catch-22 created by the enrollment decline. With the numbers down, staff members were reluctant to expel disruptive students. But the enrollment kept falling, in part because a few kids were so unruly, and parents were worried about their children's safety. It was a hard decision, but early on, Sister Constance expelled a few troublemakers. We had to set standards. We had to be tough at first so we could loosen up later. Nobody can teach when kids disrupt the class.

Word began to spread. We know that children will stretch the limits when they think they can get away with something. We firmed up the behavioral boundaries, and things began to change.

DIFFICULT LIVES

The third big challenge was of a very different nature from money needs and discipline issues, and much more important. Many children who were coming to St. Francis had an accumulation of hurt, anger, and sadness—the result of terrible experiences that we could only imagine. Some had lived in refugee camps. Some had witnessed rapes of family members and worse. Others had walked long, exhausting, and dangerous miles to freedom. Their beautiful faces, haunting eyes, and stoic solemnity hid many horrific memories. It was heartbreaking.

Konowa, who came from Sierra Leone, was often absent, but when he wasn't, he sat all day uninvolved and impassive. His seventh-grade teachers tried to engage him with his work and summoned his father for a conference, but nothing changed. Finally, his father told the teachers that Konowa had been forced to be a child soldier in the Sierra Leone Civil War and had killed many people—and he could not get those images out of his mind. The father eventually took Konowa out of school and moved away.

Some of our Amerasian children had spent their earlier childhood in post-war Vietnam and had been belittled and demeaned. One young boy, the child of a Vietnamese mother and an American soldier, acted like a beaten dog. Psychologically destroyed by his earlier experiences, he showed no affect and lacked any confidence. You could see the despair on his young face. We wished we could hug him and promise that things would change, but his body language denied even the possibility. It was not long before his family left Philadelphia.

In the 1980s, thousands of families were still making their way to the United States from Southeast Asia—a lasting impact of the Vietnam War. It seemed that all of the maps pointed to St. Francis de Sales, which to this day remains the home parish to the Philadelphia Vietnamese community. About 40 percent of our students at that time were refugees—mainly Vietnamese, Cambodian, Laotian, and Hmong. Many families were sending money back to Vietnam's Communist government to try to buy freedom for loved ones left behind.

Our school community had been unprepared for so many children who didn't speak English and arrived in the United States with just the clothes on their backs. They were likely to show up on their first day of school in flip-flops, a thin dress or shirt, often without underwear. The parish, however, did have a large collection of donated clothes available to families. We also kept items that kids could use to meet the school's dress code.

> *Many of the families who were flown from the refugee camps located in Asia to Philadelphia landed at night, and then were taken to overcrowded apartment buildings in our neighborhood.*
>
> *One day, a fifth-grade teacher took a group of students on the subway to visit the Free Library of Philadelphia in Center City. When the children came up from the subway underground and saw the flowing fountains, flowers, and imposing buildings, Duong exclaimed to his teacher, "Mr. Clay, I know we came to America for freedom, but I did not know that it was also beautiful!"*

Over the years, immigrant children—most of them refugees—continued to account for about 40 percent of our enrollment, but their native countries changed. As Asian families worked hard, prospered, and left the neighborhood, refugees from Africa moved in. Initially, many were fleeing the Ethiopian-Eritrean War. Later, we enrolled children from Sierra Leone, Mali, Liberia, and elsewhere. The remainder of the student body was predominantly African American—a reflection of the neighborhood's changing demographics.

Sister Jeannette:

> *There are certain experiences with the children that you never forget. You put Catholic school uniforms on children, and they all look similar. Sometimes you might not realize what has happened to them or the situations they now endure before and after school.*

> *I remember one child who had an accident in class. Of course, we had extra pants and underwear handy. We cleaned up the child and placed his soiled pants and underwear in a bag for his older sister to take home to wash. She later explained that she couldn't wash the clothes because their home was without water.*

BUILDING COMMUNITY

Sister Constance:

> *My fundamental task for the first year was to get to know the whole situation—listening, watching, observing. I was in search of what would work here, what I could latch onto to energize the faculty and children. We tried so hard to encourage the children, to get them excited about themselves—so hard that*

early on a child asked me, "Are you a cheerleader or the new principal?"

One thing I was determined to do was hold a Back-to-School night. The teachers said, "Oh, we don't have parent meetings; nobody will come." To which I said, "But we're supposed to welcome these children and their parents. That is our role."

We held the Back-to School night in the auditorium, just as I had at St. Agnes, my previous school in the suburbs. We set up displays of the new books and materials the kids would be using and put out a sign-up sheet for parents who wanted to volunteer at the school. We also provided a suggestion box, though I discovered later that some parents had no idea why it was there. One of the first suggestions: "God bless the teachers."

Our parents filled the auditorium. THEY DID COME! (When large numbers of refugee families arrived at the school, we tried to hold special nights for them.)

We started by enthusiastically thanking them for coming and for sending their children to our school. We made clear that we were delighted to have them. Then we introduced each of the teachers and invited the parents to walk with their children's teachers to their classrooms. Most of these parents had never been invited into the school, let alone into their children's classrooms.

Language, of course, was a barrier, so we had different Back-to-School nights for American and Southeast Asian families. No one on the staff spoke Laotian or Thai, but the faculty included two

Vietnamese Christian Brothers who taught our newest arrivals from Southeast Asia. This was part of the services provided under the *Indochina Migration and Refugee Assistance Act* of 1975.

Brother Phuong was young, peppy, and outgoing—and very tough on the students, which evidently was the way it was done in Vietnam. Brother Cosmas was older and had a hard time handling the little ones. In addition to instructing the children, the Brothers helped educate the two of us.

For example, we had wondered why the Vietnamese children would never meet our gaze. Brother Phuong explained that in Vietnam it is disrespectful for a child to look an adult in the eye.

This photo of the school's Southeast Asian students was taken in 1988. Brother Phuong is on the left of the first standing row and Brother Cosmas on the right.

APPRECIATING DIVERSITY

Encouraging multi-ethnic appreciation in the school community was another of our priorities early on. Up to that time, there had not been much recognition of the students' different cultures. Once we started to celebrate the children's national and ethnic backgrounds, the school environment began to change.

Sister Jeannette:

Children new to America want to be just like everyone else, but I firmly believe that denying who you are does not need to be part of that transition. We had students who didn't want their parents to meet with us because they were embarrassed that their parents did not speak English. It hurt my heart to see that happen. Also, lots of children changed their names when they moved here, but I would always refer to them by their given names—even when those names were hard to pronounce.

Children don't want to be different, but it seemed important that our kids be proud of their roots, not embarrassed by them. So, I sent away for a large map of the world and when it arrived, I asked the children to point to their countries of origin.

I remember the first student pointed to Eritrea and the second pointed to Ethiopia. The two boys told about those troubled East African nations from their perspectives. We discussed the fact that Ethiopia is land-locked while Eritrea has access to water, and the children were able to surmise some of the reasons for the ongoing conflict. As time went on, children from Ethiopia and Eritrea became best friends even though their parents had fought one another back home. "Never Kneel Down Eritrea" was a common bumper sticker on neighborhood cars at the time.

We used an old overhead projector to enlarge the countries that the students came from so they could pinpoint their specific home areas. I gave out lengths of yarn and had the children use the yarn to trace their journeys to the United States. Once a "yarn trail" was glued in place, all the students from that country printed their names around it.

They loved the exercise. It was as if they had never before really thought about where their classmates came from. The room was filled with 'Wows' and 'Ohs' as the students recruited children from other classrooms to watch the yarn pieces multiply. Over time, children from all over the school became part of our yarn-trail geography lesson. I can still see the young girl with straight black hair, a long thin nose, and caramel-colored skin so eager for someone else to sign next to her name so she wouldn't have to represent her country all by herself. Finally, another Sri Lankan child came forth from a lower grade!

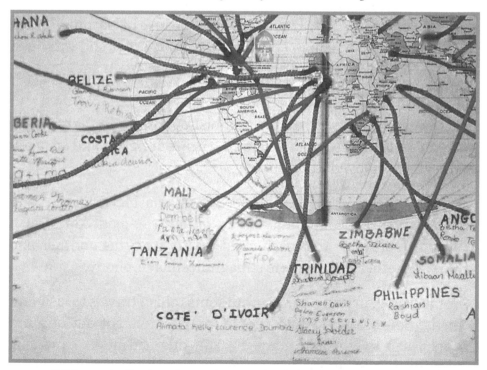

Children proudly signed near the yarn that led to their country of origin.

The completed map was amazing, and from it emerged a new awareness. A girl inquired about the meaning of a classmate's name and asked that he write it on the blackboard. He did, explaining that it meant "strong." Immediately, other kids began to tell the significance of their names. And as the foreign-born kids began sharing their stories, many of our native-born American students were amazed to learn that people in other countries not only spoke different languages but wrote with entirely different alphabet characters. No wonder it was so difficult to learn.

The Archbishop of Philadelphia visited the school during *National Migration Month* one year. To mark the occasion, we had a celebration where the children announced their nations' various gifts to their new homeland:

"I am from the island of Haiti, and we bring the gift of song and dance." "I am from Vietnam, and the gift we bring is strong family life." "I am from Eritrea, and we share the love of learning." As each child spoke, a large map of his or her country of origin was hoisted high. The last child said simply, "I am from the USA. The gift we offer is welcome."

At the end of the program, the Archbishop rose and announced, "My family is from Italy, and the gifts we bring are pizza and spaghetti." The children loved it!

While some refer to the United States as a melting pot, we like to describe our community as an orchestra—made up of all the beautiful customs that each child brings from his and her native land. Together they became a magnificent symphony.

Some of our African American students told of travels to visit family in the South where white people immediately got out of a motel pool when they would jump in. Our kids had never experienced prejudice at St. Francis because, as one child said, "*everyone* is different here."

CHILDREN'S STORIES: The Importance of Listening

Another lesson we learned early on was that even if our children did not have the language skills to express themselves, they needed an outlet for their memories. Oftentimes, they began a sentence with "But Sister...," and we began to understand that if we let them speak, we would hear things we'd never heard before. They needed to tell their stories.

Our philosophy of education began to center on drawing out the children. We gave them paper and pencils to write about or sketch their experiences so the pain could begin to find its way out of their minds and hearts. We always listened.

Sister Jeannette:

> *Several Southeast Asian children wrote about pirates—real pirates who waited in rivers or the open sea for families escaping by boat. The pirates knew that women hid jewelry in the hems of their clothes and would rip off the clothes of mothers and sisters and rape them right in front of our children.*
>
> *One student, whom we will call Thanh (not his real name), always looked like an old man—serious, head bowed, eyes troubled. Thanh wrote about the desperate thirst he and family members experienced when they ran out of water on the open sea during their escape. He told of an uncle who went mad from thirst, jumped into the sea, and was eaten by a large fish (shark?).*
>
> *Thanh escaped and made it to Philadelphia*

with his brothers and a sister. But his father, mother, and a little brother remained in Vietnam.

> In 1987 I arrived in U.S. now I lived with my brothers and my sister. My father and my mother and my little brother still in Vietnam. Sometime I thinking about my family. I am very sad, because every my friends, they <u>have</u> mother and family lived with them.

"Sometime I thinking about my family," he wrote. "I am very sad because every my friends they have mother and family lived with them."

Thanh's story has a sad ending. He made it through high school, but in his second year at Temple University, he suffered a heart attack and died. I have always believed he died of a broken heart, having endured such misery in his young life. His parents never did escape from Vietnam.

There were so many tales. One could almost read them on those young faces, behind those often-troubled eyes. And so, we continued to listen. Choun wrote the story of his family's attempted escape from Cambodia. When he recorded his heart-breaking true story, he was thirteen years old and in my eighth-grade class.

I REMEMBER THE MOUNTAIN by Choun Ea

When the day finally came, I didn't even know about the mountain that awaited us. My family and many others had been in the refugee camp in Thailand for more than six months. Children, unaware of what was about to happen, played outside as they did every day while parents and young adults packed a few necessities. There was excitement in the packing, yet tension. Unexpectedly, a voice rang out of a bullhorn. Everyone listened as directions were being given. The names of heads of families were called. These families were to board the bus, which would take them to the airport. As each name was called, my parents grew more and more tense. When my uncle and grandmother were called, they stepped on the bus then turned and looked warily at us. Finally, all the buses had gone, except one. When the last name for that bus had been called, it was not ours! We and hundreds of others were left. In alarm and confusion, we wondered, "What is going to happen to us?" Although I was young, I was able to sense these feelings. Everyone was motionless. The silence was so deep I could hear hearts beat as loudly as drums. I picked up a rhythm in the heartbeats, a rhythm I had heard before. It was a rhythm of confusion mixed with dejected anger, and most of all, fear. There is a kind of fear that seems to pierce slowly through the heart. On the faces around me, I remember seeing that kind of fear.

The next thing we knew, soldiers advanced toward us pointing guns. By now the adults realized what was happening. They put the children in the center crowded together. Then our mothers surrounded us. Next, the adult men formed the outer circle, holding hands around us. The soldiers stepped toward us, their faces bare of *all emotion. They closed in and tried to pull the men's hands apart, but they couldn't. The soldiers' muscles were nothing compared with the strength of our hearts and wills. When they realized our determination, the soldiers began to speak to us calmly. They assured us that our fear of being returned to Cambodia was unfounded. Instead, they explained that we had been selected to go to Bangkok, Thailand's largest city. There we would be free to choose to become Thai citizens or to fly to the United States. The soldiers pointed to several buses, which had just pulled up. At the mercy of hope, we trusted them. We boarded the buses...*

As we rode for several hours, my father's doubts grew. He had been to Bangkok before, and this wasn't the way. But neither he nor any other passenger on that bus had the courage to stand up to the immense pain of the truth. The people forced themselves to believe the soldiers because they weren't strong enough to accept reality. Each of us begged in our hearts to be hugged by arms that promised hope. While we rode, darkness began to fall. As the sun faded, so did our hope. It was very early the next morning when the bus stopped at the foot of the mountain. The soldiers didn't tell us what mountain this was or where it led. They just commanded us to cross it. Blinded by hope, our desperate determination to live in freedom in a nation with a promising future, and lacking knowledge of the area, we did as ordered.

It was a cool, windy morning. The red sun had just escaped the horizon. I remember a strange scent carried to us by a light wind. As we walked, the scent grew stronger and stronger. We turned a curve in the road.

Horrified, we saw the source of the smell. Rotted bodies! Men, women, children—refugees like ourselves. Then we realized we were being forced <u>back</u> into Cambodia. The bodies had the most horrifying looks on their faces in death. They seemed to have been pleading with their gods to save them. I couldn't stand this dreadful sight, but couldn't ignore it either. Those faces were warning us of danger. We began to run back toward the buses, but the soldiers stood there shooting at us. We had no choice but to turn and continue on the path, no choice but to step over the bodies covered with blood like sheets of red blankets. We knew we had to walk slowly and cautiously on a very narrow path. Those in front showed where they thought land mines were buried. But eventually, thirst siphoned life away. Desperately searching for water, many people forgot to be careful and stepped on bombs. Many others, usually the old or very young, died of starvation.

I describe this mountain journey as full of despondency and despair, but the meaning of these words can <u>never</u> describe its dreadfulness. However, for the sake of their children, for the sake of survival, my parents and others were determined to go on.

I remember a new fear the day we met a group of Vietnamese soldiers. They considered us betrayers of the Communist system for leaving Cambodia. They threatened to kill us. Some who knew how to speak Vietnamese begged and pleaded with them. They told the soldiers of our struggle on the mountain and bitterness we had endured. We looked helplessly at the commander while he decided. After a time, he had compassion on us. He not only agreed to let us go, but even ordered his men to help us dig up some of the deadly mines. Some of the Vietnamese lost their lives for us.

After we crossed the Cambodian border, we had more hardships. Day after day we walked through forests and wilderness. We were without shelter when the rains came. We slept under trees, which didn't offer much protection. Our feet had splinters and were swollen. Sometimes we wrapped rags around them to lessen the pain.

My little sister, Chy, who was six, walked with the rest of us. One evening, we were so exhausted, we forgot to check on Chy. When darkness came, we stopped to rest and realized that she wasn't with us. My father went in search of her. He was exhausted and fearful. Later, he told us the wolves' howls sounded as if they were very close to him. He gripped a wooden club to defend himself. Then he heard footsteps dragging along the dirt trail. Unable to see in the darkness, he called her name. After a few seconds, my sister responded, "Pa! Pa!" They grabbed each other with relief. With what was left of his strength, my father carried Chy back to us.

There was more joy when, after days of walking, we finally reached a city. Here we thought we could survive. We found an abandoned house with one floor and an attic. Dust nearly buried the house. The walls were cracked. The floor boards were rotted. We made this our home. To get food for us, my father began to buy rice, then trade it for chickens. He then traded the chickens to the soldiers of the invading Vietnamese army for rice. With each trade, he got a little more back. Still, all of us had to work. My mother made little cakes and sold them at the street market. Chy and I also sold these little cakes along the streets. Sometimes people snatched things away from us without our noticing. Khmer Rouge soldiers frequently searched our house while we were gone and took what we had. Because of this, we hid our rice and few belongings in the attic.

One evening when we came home, my mother went to the attic to get rice. She carefully made her way across the weakened floor. But she slipped as the boards crunched and broke and she fell through. I think I sucked up every bit of air in the house as I watched her fall. I was frozen motionless, couldn't move. My brain was screaming and shouting commands to my body, but I was cast under a spell of immobility. When I finally got to her, she was trying to move. I looked into her eyes and saw the devastating pain that tortured her. She tried to gasp for air, then suddenly stopped moving completely. We rushed her to a place where she would receive medical help. As we waited to see if she would recover, I wondered what would happen to her. She was the one who loved me more than anyone, who had let me eat more than she when we were starving in the Communist labor camp, in the Thailand refugee camp, and on the mountain. She was the one who encouraged me when I wanted to give up, who comforted my deepest fears. She was the one _I_ loved more than anyone else in the world. As I thought of these things, tears burst *from my heart, tears that felt hotter than fire, tears that burned my cheeks as they poured down. During the weeks that followed, she suffered a painful paralysis. Discouragement almost overcame me as I stayed with her and cared for her. Only her gradual and painful recovery eventually calmed my sorrow.*

During this time though, my father found new work that brought us more rice. Each day he led a group of men to cut bamboo for the Vietnamese soldiers. From them he heard news that the United Nations had <u>now</u> agreed to support any Cambodians who would be able to escape to Thailand! My parents talked about this news late into the night. The next morning, they told my sister and me that our family was going to try again. We would travel <u>back across the mountain</u> into Thailand. Maybe this time we would get to the United States. I paused and stared at them. A freezing cold fear chilled my body when I heard the decision. I remembered too well that last trip across the mountain. The horrifying faces of the dead appeared often in my mind. I protested, "We are doing fine here. We have enough to eat. Dad has work." But my mother said, "There is one thing we do not have, Choun. We do not have freedom." She explained that the work my father did put him in grave danger if caught by the Khmer Rouge. After hearing the reasons, I understood better. My father traded the bags of rice we had saved for gold, which he used to pay for a truck ride to the border of Cambodia.

As we rode in the truck <u>back toward that terrible mountain</u>, I asked myself again and again if we had made the right choice. Were we deceiving ourselves?

Could our dream of a free life possibly survive more danger? I thought of the mountain, and I knew the future lay in its shadow. Yet, I also knew that we had found strength to cross it before. Together we would walk on; we would face the mountain together!

A friend once gave us winter coats to give the children, and one coat went to an Eritrean girl named Eden. Lacking paper at home, Eden used the coat box lid to draw a picture of her grass-roofed home in Africa and to tell about her life there. The next day she brought the embellished box to school as her way of saying thank you. We have treasured it, misspellings and all, for more than three decades.

I was in AEFRICA I lived near the river, ground and the Mountens. I lived in a small hut. The people had farm, and some animals like dog, goat, ship, cow, horse dankey All these animals used in the farm, and in the village. Around the village it's has nice trees, corns, and fruit and other foods. The people working in the ground to feed the roots they feeding wate. by backet and They had truck to drive the trees and other things like milk, foods, and animals to take from the village to the city and other places to help the people. The weather in the village is natural no cold no wear it is very, very. nice air on it it is beautifuly to live it. I hope to come back on it. my family are lived in the village they had fun time on it the liked to live in there they had long time on it and they liked very, very, will they now how the people act and systen in work time and in the life.

> *I was in Africa. I lived near the river, ground and the mountens. I lived in a small hut. The people had farm, and some animals like dog, goat, ship, cow, horse, dankey. All these animals used in the farm and in the village. Around the village it's has nice trees, corns, and fruit and other foods. The people working in the ground to feed the roots. They feeding water by backet and they had truck to drive the trees and other things like milk, foods and animals to take from the village to the city and other places to help the people. The weather in the village is natural no cold no wear. It is very, very nice air on it. It is beautifuly to live it. I hope to come back on it. My family are lived in the village. They had fun time on it. They liked to live in there. They had long time on it and they liked very, very will. They know how the people act and system in work time and in the life.*

My Family đồng hut
mái cái pilgrums. Mừn
đổ cái tou để qua
my cho freedom.

My Family is like the
pilgrums.
We went in a boat to
America for freedom

The first four lines written by Vietnamese student Chien may be difficult to decipher, but the meaning of the last four could not be clearer. The journeys undertaken by so many thousands took every bit of courage they could muster.

SISTER MIRIAM: A 'Unique' Communicator

All of us on the staff tried hard to relate to our diverse school community, but try as we might, intercultural communications did not always go smoothly.

We arrived at St. Francis at the same time as Sister Miriam Agnes. She was the new superior in the Convent and also assisted in the school office. With her beautiful face and bright blue dancing eyes, she was a great blessing to the convent. She enjoyed life, and there was always laughter when she was around.

In the school office, however, Sister Miriam was serious, and you never knew what she might say. She also never seemed to grasp the concept of people speaking another language, which made registering new arrivals from Southeast Asia and other foreign countries a challenge. She was quite willing to help them fill out their forms. It was no trouble copying names and birth dates from a passport. But when it came to religion, problems could arise.

Sister Miriam would start by asking in a normal voice, "Are you Catholic?" The poor parent who spoke no English would murmur something in languages like Vietnamese, Khmer, Thai, or Urdu. Her volume increasing, Sister would then ask, "Are you baptized?" No response. Things hit high decibels as Sister screamed, "DO YOU BELIEVE IN GOD?" When that didn't work, she would just write "Buddhist" on the registration form. Even with the help of Brother Phuong, it took us months to straighten out our records.

One consequence of Sister Miriam's office reign came home some years later. Meron, an eighth-grade student, was filling out papers for admission to West Catholic High School and asked if he should use his *real* name or his *St. Francis de Sales* name.

That's when we learned that for eight years we had been calling him by his uncle's name (Habte) instead of his own (Ghebremariam). It seems the uncle, who initially registered the child, had taken Sister Miriam's direction literally to write down *HIS name*. And nobody, including the child, ever said otherwise.

A family one day after arriving from the Democratic Republic of Congo—and then making a trip to the attic for the necessary school uniforms.

CULTURE AND COMMUNITY

Culture and community are two different things. St. Francis de Sales includes many cultures, but together we form one community. The recent funeral of Ningh Tran, the school's long-time janitor, brought that home.

Ningh, who died in 2014, had been a teacher in his native Vietnam. Back there, he would tell us, "God was first, the teacher was second, and parents were third." So, settling for the job of janitor in his new country was not easy. Over the years, however, Ningh's connection to St. Francis became a close one. All eight of his children attended the school. One of them, daughter Nguyet, who was born in the United States, ended up marrying a classmate, John, whom she met in first grade.

At Ningh's funeral service, his Irish American son-in-law wore a white cloth around his forehead—a tradition at Vietnamese burial ceremonies—and speaking for the family, thanked the church congregation and school on behalf of "our father."

Among the mourners was Rahat, originally from Bangladesh, who attended St. Francis with John and Nguyet and remains close to them. These three bright adults—from very different ethnic backgrounds—graduated more than two decades ago, and here they were together. Rahat had driven the 50+ miles from Princeton,

New Jersey, to give his support to Nguyet and John. (Rahat is a special assistant to the attorney general of New Jersey and recently married Chi-Ser, a de Sales grad whose parents escaped the Khmer Rouge in Cambodia.)

That's community, and that's what St. Francis de Sales is about.

John, holding his and Nguyet's daughter Alison, joins Sister Jeannette, Nguyet's cousin David, classmate Rahat, and Nguyet after the Funeral Mass for Nguyet's father, Ningh.

Literally from **A** to **Z**: These were the countries represented by St. Francis students and their parents in 1997. The list changed constantly depending on world conditions.

Angola	Egypt	India	Nigeria
Antigua	El Salvador	Ireland	Panama
Belize	England	Jamaica	Philippines
Burkina Faso	Eritrea	Japan	Puerto Rico
Cambodia	Ethiopia	Kenya	Senegal
Cameroon	Germany	Korea	Sierra Leone
China	Ghana	Laos	St. Vincent
Côte d'Ivoire	Guinea	Liberia	Thailand
Dominica	Great Britain	Mali	Trinidad
Dominican Republic	Guatemala	Mauritania	United States
Congo	Guyana	Mexico	Vietnam
Costa Rica	Haiti	Niger	Zimbabwe

A GRADUATE LOOKS BACK:

Choun (Jun) Ea '87
Author of "The Mountain" story in Chapter 2

Choun (Jun) Ea, 42, lives in Jersey City, New Jersey. He attended St. Francis de Sales for only one grade—the eighth.

—

We were gathered in the church for the graduation ceremony. My father had driven to Philly from the Bronx to attend. I was excited. I loved de Sales. I had only started there the previous autumn, yet so many good things had happened. I had the most remarkable teacher, Sister Jeannette, and I had made some very good friends. Although I wasn't fully aware of it at the time, I had just lived one of the most wonderful years of my life.

The previous year had been a polar contrast. We lived in the Bronx, where my parents had opened a small food store that serviced the Southeast Asian community. I found everything about the Bronx threatening. The public school I was in was a crippled institution where the teachers struggled for tenuous control of the classroom. There were fights every day. There was certainly bullying, and being one of the few Asians, I was a constant target for verbal slights. I remember having to muster every atom of courage within to get through each school day.

I don't know how I was able to convey to my parents the depth of my misery, but they got enough of it to pack me to Philadelphia the next school year to live with my uncle. So in the fall of 1985, I found myself most improbably at a Catholic school—a thing I had not known existed—about a hundred miles away from the watch of my parents.

Sister Jeannette could be a tough girl when needed. My first clear memory of her was being caught out of uniform the first week. We were queued up in the school yard before entering the building when she spotted me in a pair of aqua blue parachute pants. She approached and sternly explained to me the required clothing. Then, to my shock and embarrassment, she made me go home to change. The walk to school was over a mile. So that day, I walked over 5 miles to school and fro. I didn't repeat that mistake.

Some weeks into the year, she gave us an assignment to write a poem. I don't remember having a fluke of knowledge about poetry. I'm not even sure I had read one. But I did the assignment and turned in a free verse about the hardship of my prior year in the Bronx. I believe that that poem was the window into which she peered and gleaned various facets of me. And it would be at and through this window that she approached me—to engage, encourage, and challenge.

She asked me to stay after school to revise the poem. And this would become another of my enduring memories of St. Francis de Sales—sitting in that classroom, writing, thinking, and dreaming as Sister Jeannette flitted about her various tasks. She submitted the poem to a contest. I subsequently wrote and submitted two essays. Happily, and to my surprise, they were all received with distinction.

While it takes a sensitive and empathic teacher to look through the window of a student's heart and mind, I think it requires someone with immense passion to insist that *window remain open.*

I remember certain Saturdays and Sundays when I met with my good friend and classmate, Futsum, on the school grounds. Futsum was from Eritrea, a country utterly distant geographically and culturally from my birthplace, Cambodia. Remarkably, we often ran into Sister Jeannette going about her doings. She would pause to chat with us. While I hardly recall the substance of those conversations, I remember that her presence invariably had the effect of facilitating my friendship with Futsum.

I learned much about Futsum in those conversations in the de Sales school yard. Sister J often inquired into memories of our birth countries and the journeys that brought us here. She was concerned about our adjustment to America and whether we were able to reconcile the disparities between our new and former lives. I have not encountered another teacher before or since who demonstrated such interest.

In the 1980s and 1990s, the inner-city areas of Philadelphia were among the places in the Unites States where hopeful, ambitious, courageous, and desperate peoples from the far corners of the world landed. Whether or not they intended to, Sisters Constance and Jeannette created a space that acknowledged and honored the unique challenges facing the children of these various immigrant communities.

These challenges include the perception as well as the actuality of exclusion from the mainstream of American society, the perception and actuality of being second- or even third- class citizens, and the perception and actuality of having lesser existential worth than the dominant Caucasian majority.

Moreover, immigrant children may be required to do certain things or behave in a certain manner by their family while pressed to conform to the norm of their new society. These are not small things to expect from children. And yet they have had to do so with little or no guidance.

De Sales provided sanctuary for the children of these peoples to root themselves, find safety, uncover personal courage, and be affirmed in their self-worth. Sister Jeannette gave me the courage to ask the questions I needed to ask about myself, about the country I came from, what happened there and why, and about this country, my new home.

Though St. Francis is a Catholic school, I don't recall ever being ushered toward Catholicism or even Christianity in any degree. Rather, every word that was ever spoken to me was meant to inspire me simply to be a better person.

I only had the fortune to be there for one year, but by extrapolation, if a handful of students was blessed through these decades with experiences similar to mine, I would say that a true and profound miracle has been taking place in Philadelphia.

My enduring image of Sister Jeannette is an energetic, clear-eyed woman, deeply grounded in the realness of the moment. Yet when I think back to that year, I see a kind of magic in the way things transpired. I was doing things that I had not even imagined doing, let alone excel at. Doors of possibility and opportunity open.

I remember at the graduation when awards and honors were announced, there was a point where I was walking up and down the aisle continuously to receive them. The purpose of this telling is not to bask in the memory but to further evidence the magic that Sister Jeannette facilitated for me. and, I believe, for her many students through the years.

CHAPTER THREE

"Do it Better": Empowering Students

We wanted to build up the kids' self-esteem and talked a lot about how to do that. Principals receive numerous mailings about contests for every grade level. Most teachers did not take up the challenge, so Sister Jeannette became the official contest coordinator. She would enter the students in as many inter-scholastic contests as possible.

When our students won their first competition, Father Hilferty, the parish pastor, asked if there were any other schools in the competition. Such were the expectations of St. Francis de Sales children. (Father Hilferty, we quickly add, became one of our strongest supporters.)

After our students began winning numerous awards, some people said, "Oh, you won because you have a lot of Asian students." Then, when we had few Asian students and still won, it was, "Well, it's because you have all those *fill-in-the-blank* students."

That, of course, was way off the mark. All children can be good at something, no matter their background, if they can see possibilities for them to be successful. Defying stereotypes is what we were all about.

Sister Jeannette:

> *My father was a perfectionist who always pushed me and my brothers and sisters. He once entered me in a bicycle contest where the prize was a boy's bike. I guess I've inherited a bit of that. By the way, I won the bike!*
>
> *In my previous years as a teacher, I always challenged students to enter contests outside of the school setting; it motivated them. I introduced contests to St. Francis de Sales because I wanted the children there to have something to work toward and successes to celebrate.*
>
> *I've always demanded the best a child can do. I can see that kids are happy when they accomplish something, especially something that seems out of reach. And entering all kinds of contests brings out talents they never knew they had.*
>
> *In my first year at St. Francis, the theme chosen for the National History Day contest was "Triumph and Tragedy." It immediately jumped out at me: we had hundreds of kids whose families had triumphed over personal tragedies. Two boys in my eighth-grade class were Exhibit A.*

PURE GIFT

Adnan's family had been a victim of the turmoil surrounding the independence movement in Bangladesh. Quiet, gentle, and humble, Adnan was also determined and purposeful. His dark skin, dark hair, and the beginnings of facial hair made him seem older than he was: 14 at the time.

Chhunak, whose family had lived through the killing fields of Pol Pot's Cambodia, shared Adnan's dark hair and dark eyes. But his skin seemed somehow stretched—the result of his years of deprivation, we assumed. He and his family had suffered intensely at the hands of soldiers in the work camps. His grandmother had starved to death, he told us.

For the National History Day contest, it wasn't enough that Adnan and Chhunak had lived through the experiences about which they were writing; they also needed to put together the documentation to fulfill the criteria for the contest. For that, we gave them trolley tokens to take the number 34 line to the University of Pennsylvania Library.

Today we wouldn't let them go by themselves, and the university wouldn't let them take out books. But back then there were no such barriers—just two boys' desire to learn as much as they could. Although English was not their first language, they plowed through many Penn library books and produced their contest entries.

Adnan's was a research paper: *Triumph over Tragedy: The Birth of Bangladesh*. Chhunak's project was a magnificent rendering of his country's most sacred site and his family's escape, titled *Angkor Wat: A Holy Place Defiled*. Chhunak had once visited Angkor Wat:

> *"My father wanted me to see this holy place. I didn't know why he chose that time but realized later that he was planning to escape—but couldn't tell us kids. He felt his oldest son should have knowledge of our heritage."*

Chhunak's drawing of the national shrine was done with a very fine pen. When an artist in the parish declared him an expert in pointillism, Chhunak, who had no idea what pointillism was, explained that he simply thought the drawing would look "softer" that way.

ANGKOR WAT:
A HOLY PLACE DEFILED.

Chhunak's rendering of the Angkor Wat temple complex is unbelievably detailed. Side panels depict the temple location and some of his memories of the time he and his brother spent in Pol Pot's Khmer Rouge work camp.

As soon as I saw it, I told him, "Make another one just like it that we can enter in another contest." Chhunak arrived the next day with a second Angkor Wat rendering, which went on to win first place in the Archdiocesan Art Contest. We later visited his home and learned that he created these works of art while leaning on a thin mattress on the floor, with an electric bulb dangling above—it had taken him the whole night to recreate his masterpiece.

The National History Day contest rules required that all entered paperwork be computer-generated. But we had no computer. A friend heard of our predicament and reproduced the students' entries on his dot-matrix printer. As we proofread Adnan's paper, we noticed a spelling mistake. "Not a problem," said Chhunak. With great precision, he reconstructed the dots to form the correct letter, and no one ever knew the difference. Chhunak never had an art lesson in his life. How can this be? Pure gift!

A LONG JOURNEY

The first stage of the competition was in March and drew students in grades 6–12 from Philadelphia and the four surrounding counties. Hundreds of people—students, their teachers, and parents—filled an auditorium at Temple University. Like a science fair, the entries were all on display, and the students defended theirs as the bevy of judges moved up and down the aisles.

At one point, the judges were within earshot, and we overheard one say, "*They* are the primary sources for their work. They have their stamped passports and the *actual documents* from the camps!" We suspected they were talking about our two boys.

At the end of that day, Adnan and Chhunak each received first-place ribbons and advanced to the Pennsylvania state finals at Penn State University. One of the judges was overheard saying that Adnan's was the best research paper he had ever read!

In mid-May, the two of us drove the two scholars the 200 miles to Penn State. The boys stayed in a dorm, and we checked into a nearby motel. The competition began on Ascension Thursday, and we told the boys, one Muslim, the other Buddhist, that it was a holy day for us and we wouldn't be able to pick them up until after Mass the next morning. They told us not to worry, one adding, "No matter what name we use, the same God loves us all."

Adnan and Chhunak were both soft spoken, and we worried they might be reluctant to defend their work. The judges pushed all of the contestants hard to make sure they had produced their projects themselves, not their parents or teachers. When the judges questioned our students, it was clear they had done every bit of it themselves! They knew exactly what they were talking about because they had *lived* it.

I remember hearing people talk to one another about Chhunak's project, which included photos of his grandparents, the family nameplate from the barracks in the refugee camp, and the papers admitting them to the United States. The film *The Killing Fields* had come out only a few months earlier, and people were fascinated by the story.

The final result at States: Two first-place ribbons!

The third leg of the competition—the Nationals—took us to the University of Maryland, College Park campus just outside D.C. We couldn't afford to stay overnight for the three days, so we drove back and forth from Philadelphia each day, about a two-and-a-half hour drive each way.

I recall the first morning, stopping for breakfast somewhere along I-95. As soon as they got their menus, we could see that Adnan and Chhunak had never eaten an American breakfast. We tried to explain the food items and what utensils to use. These boys were both so humble; goodness shown through their eyes. Perhaps that's what tremendous suffering can do to you.

During our time together, Chhunak told us of Pol Pot's voice being piped into the labor camps constantly, haranguing them as they sat for hours on hard logs forced to listen to his lectures. "I heard people being tortured at night at the temples, and I did bad things. I smashed the statues of Buddha," he told us, as if confessing.

Sister Constance responded that if the soldiers made you do these things, then you had no choice. That seemed to give him some comfort, though we suspect these memories were close to his consciousness much of the time. Chhunak often suffered from headaches, though he never complained.

Nationals was a new adventure for us all. Now their work was in competition with students from all over the United States. Although the two stuck pretty close to us, they met and mingled with some of the brightest young scholars in the country.

FATHER HILFERTY: Beginning to Believe

Adnan and Chhunak knew there would be students from all over the United States, but they seemed surprised that they all dressed similarly. For some reason, our boys thought they would be able to recognize the students' home states by the clothing they wore, since that was the case in their countries. Perhaps it was an impression picked up from some map of the nation that featured Texans in cowboy boots and Coloradans in mining gear. Our boys wore inexpensive suits from a local thrift store or borrowed from another family; the suits were tight and worn, the pants a bit too short.

The pressure built over the three days, but Adnan and Chhunak remained calm through every interview. The two of <u>us</u> were the ones anxious and bursting inside. When the judging wrapped up, thousands of people gathered in the field house to hear the results.

There were balloons and banners everywhere. Our Pennsylvania state delegation included hopeful contestants, their teachers, and their parents from every area of the Commonwealth all gathered in the area around the *'You've Got a Friend in Pennsylvania'* banner.

The PA delegation at History Day Nationals. In the front row: L to R: Adnan (dark blue suit and tie), Chhunak (holding flag), Sister Jeannette and Sister Constance.

Contest officials stood at the center of the stage and announced the winners, beginning with honorable mention. Oh, the excitement: flashbulbs popping, pictures being taken, balloons being released.

Sister Jeannette:

> *In the Project category, Chhunak received 3rd place and $250, and we were pleasantly surprised that the judges pronounced his name correctly. As his teacher, I all but floated up to the stage with him. I admit I had to keep from screaming out while he politely shook hands, turned, and walked calmly back to his seat.*
>
> *The first-place ribbon for the Best Research Paper and a check for $1,000 went to Adnan. Imagine how shocked the audience was to see the same nun come up again with a different student to claim the prize. Like Chhunak, Adnan responded with a handshake and a shy smile for the cameras.*
>
> *Though reserved by nature, these two young boys made it easy to tell how excited they were—beaming as they posed with everyone who wanted pictures taken with them. By now they knew each other well, and you could see how deeply happy they were for each other.*
>
> *The ride home was glorious. All four of us were a combination of thrilled, proud, and dead tired. I guess I wasn't watching our speed, and a policeman pulled us over. This was my first offense! The officer looked inside our little blue Geo Prism, two nuns in*

the front, two sleepy students in the back, and let us off with a warning. I felt embarrassed in front of the boys, but they never said a word about it.

It was 1985, so we had no cell phones to announce our good news. Arriving back in Philadelphia late at night, we took Adnan and Chhunak to their homes, and returned to the convent. The next morning we couldn't wait to tell all the Sisters, and they shared our excitement like family. Then we walked across the street to the rectory to tell the pastor, but *The Philadelphia Inquirer*, our hometown daily paper, had beaten us to the punch. Our doubting pastor had already seen it in the newspaper: "Two Philadelphia students win prizes at National History Day Competition." Father Hilferty was beginning to believe.

Indeed, the next year, Chhunak's brother, Chhunakar, followed in his sibling's footsteps, winning first place in the National History Day's local, state, and national competitions with his own rendering of his family's escape from Cambodia.

Chhunakar's award-winning entry illustrated the violence his country suffered under Pol Pot, his workcamp interment, his family's escape, refugee camp time, and finally, their joyous arrival in the United States.

This project occasioned an important glimpse into the Cambodian culture. Sometimes Chhunakar would bring his project to school so he could work at lunchtime or after school. In the center he had drawn the map of Cambodia, and it was easy to recognize his father's face in the top left corner. Two days later, we saw to our amazement that the *grandmother's* face had replaced it. The parents had made him *erase the father* because his grandmother was the eldest, the most revered and should be first.

In March 1986, Chhunakar won the Commonwealth of Pennsylvania's Women's History Month art contest with his drawings of famous Pennsylvania women on a map of the state. We drove him to Harrisburg to receive the award from Governor Dick Thornburgh. Following the ceremony, we walked to the banks of the nearby Susquehanna River.

"This is like the river," Chhunakar murmured after a while.

"What river?" Sister Jeannette asked.

"The one in my village where the bodies floated by."

After a few moments of silence, Sister asked, "Did you see any of them killed?"

Chhunkar then told how families in Cambodia had been separated. He and his siblings were sent to a children's work camp and their parents to another camp. As laborers, the children had to kneel in the paddies and gather rice while teenage soldiers watched.

A four-year-old boy put some rice in his mouth, which was forbidden, and a young solider put a plastic bag over the little boy's head and suffocated him. The soldiers had been instructed not to waste bullets on children.

We recalled seeing mounds of blue plastic bags in the film The Killing Fields. *Now we knew why.*

Chhunakar, Pennsylvania Governor Dick Thornburg, and Sister Jeannette at the 1986 award ceremony.

A SCIENCE PROJECT: More Success

A collective eighth-grade science project led to another big win for the school early on. At the time, we were worried about how many of our students had asthma and other breathing problems—so many more, it seemed, than in other schools.

In response to a high rate of asthma in the eighth-grade class, Sister Jeannette's kids called ten other schools and charted the numbers of students with asthma along with where they lived. They documented a relationship between asthma and pollution sources. During a discussion of the problem in science class, the kids concluded that if more people would ride public transportation, the St. Francis de Sales neighborhoods would be less exposed to air pollutants and, thus, less asthma. The school is located a mere mile and a half from the traffic-choked Schuylkill Expressway. This is the most congested highway in Pennsylvania, and more than 200,000 vehicles travel it each day.

Sister Jeannette egged them on. "Well, what are we going to do about it?" The students began to call out ideas, and she wrote each one on the blackboard so there could be discussion. From there, a campaign took off.

The kids interviewed family members, neighbors, and students in other grades about pollution problems and their ideas for solving them. Then they expanded their research. From the classroom phone, they contacted different experts and organizations. From the American Lung Association, for example, they learned how many school days in the United States are lost each year due to asthma—10 million!

Working together like a think tank, they came up with all sorts of good proposals to address the reasons folks gave for not using buses, trolleys, and trains:

- Offer a free-transit Thursday to encourage people in the suburbs to take the bus and leave their cars at home. The Southeastern Pennsylvania Transit Authority—SEPTA—later implemented that very idea.

- In order to keep cost of ridership affordable, sell advertising on the <u>outside</u> of the buses. SEPTA did that, too. In fact, entire exteriors of buses became rolling advertisements for companies.

- Create bus-only lanes so buses didn't have to deal with car traffic, making riders late for work. (The city did that as well.)

Then the children organized a STEP Conference, "Students Trying to Eliminate Pollution," for December 2, 1993. Invitations went out to public transportation officials from Philadelphia and South Jersey, as well as organizations concerned with health, clean air, the environment, and regional planning. They included media as well.

The guests arrived and listened politely, passively indulging the youngsters for their efforts. Before long, however, pens and papers came out, and the audience began taking notes.

PHILADELPHIA DAILY NEWS

FRIDAY, DECEMBER 3, 1993

Kids full of ideas on transit

by **Marianne Costantinou**

Daily News Staff Writer

ALEJANDRO A. ALVAREZ/ DAILY NEWS

Students display the "Take Transit Seriously" sign they designed

They say that out of the mouths of babes come pearls of wisdom. Or something like that.

Well, the eighth-graders at St. Francis De Sales School in West Philadelphia aren't exactly babes. But yesterday, they gave public transit officials some much-needed advice.

With charts and speeches, the Catholic school pupils suggested ideas about how to get more people to ride mass transit as a way to cut pollution. The event's theme: "Take Transit Seriously."

Sitting in the audience at the school's STEP (Students Trying to Eliminate Pollution) conference were officials from SEPTA, PATCO and New Jersey Transit.

At first, the grown-ups just smiled and nodded at the students' enthusiasm. But before long, pens were pulled out of suit pockets and handbags, and the officials were taking notes.

Advertise more, the kids said. And to pay for the ads, why not tap into some of the federal money now being used by high-

ways?

Use billboards, "so people can read them while they're stuck in traffic," said one girl.

Give discount rides to city employees as a labor contract benefit, so they will leave their cars at home.

Create "Bus Only" streets so that the buses don't get stuck in traffic. Faster service will mean faithful customers.

Make buses and trains more comfortable. Add a TV set. Even a fridge.

One student suggested giving commuters a free ride for every

dozen or so. The transit system could keep track by issuing riders special computerized cards. The cards would tally the rides.

SEPTA is already working on the technology for something like that for monthly Trailpass and Transpass users, said an official.

But what about the people who use tokens? asked the student. It wouldn't be fair to exclude them.

"That was a good response," the SEPTA official whispered to the woman sitting next to him, who was from PATCO.

And he picked up his notebook again. ∎

PHILADELPHIA DAILY NEWS   FRIDAY, DECEMBER 3, 1993

12/3/93 Used with permission Philadelphia Inquirer Copyright 2018

The event was a tremendous success, and the two students who headed up the STEP committee were selected to travel to Florida to receive $5,000 plus an award as part of a television special saluting young Americans for their commitment to environmental awareness and protection.

PAGE 12   **Weekly PRESS**   JUNE 29, 1995

St. Francis De Sales Wins National Environmental Award

"The students of St. Francis De Sales School made a difference, but we're not finished yet. Our Pledge and Promise is this: mas and Sister Jeannette Lucey, IHM acknowledged their concern for the quality of air in Southwest Philadelphia and the determination of the students of St. Francis de Sales School to continue their efforts to improve it.

The Conservation Summit at Busch Gardens in Tampa, Florida culminated with the announcement of their second place national winner's standing on the June 7th, 8:00 p.m. CBS Special "Party for the Planet."

Finally, they were asked to participate in a Press Conference on September 19, 1994 along with media, transportation and government officials. Try Transit Day #2 finally arrived. There was a tremendous downpour! In spite of a typical decline on rainy days, however, SEPTA did report a gain of 10,000 riders. Although those results were somewhat disappointing, because students hoped there would be many more riders, they aren't letting it stop them. They know there's a close connection between asthma, air pollution and automobile exhaust. They believe that if all students would Try to Eliminate Pollution, there could be enough clean air to break that connec-

6/29/93 Used with permission Weekly Press

The two of us accompanied our awardees to Orlando, and as we got off the plane, we were excited to see palm trees and coconuts. The students were more excited when they saw someone wearing a Tommy Hilfiger shirt, which of course the two of us had never heard of. We all stayed in a motel—a first for the two girls—and were guests at Busch Gardens, where we were mesmerized by the giant turtles!

Today, when we see the innovations suggested by these young city planners in use throughout the SEPTA system, it makes us soooo proud.

YOU NAME IT, WE ENTERED

Sister Jeannette entered the children in every kind of contest—essay contests, math contests, geography contests, and even smile contests. You name it, we entered. Our students won competitions put on by the Daughters of the American Republic, Veterans of Foreign Wars, Mothers Against Drunk Driving, and a wide range of other organizations. Even better, the children won tens of thousands of dollars in academic scholarships.

Art contests were a major staple of the school's competition schedule.

Sister Constance:

> At award ceremonies and among parishioners and other principals, the question was often asked of me, "Who is your art teacher?" To which I would reply, "We don't have one, and Sister Jeannette doesn't know a thing about art."
>
> I recall a wonderfully talented artist, an eighth-grade girl named Chhengly who had arrived the year before from Cambodia. I saw one of her works, a beautiful drawing of Dr. Martin Luther King Jr. hanging in the hallway. His head was enshrouded in an exquisite bunch of grapes, each grape perfectly formed and looking good enough to eat. I

complimented Chhengly and asked why she chose to surround MLK with grapes. She replied proudly, "Because Sister Jeannette told us Dr. King was a grape man."

Sister Jeannette:

> *When anyone asked me what technique I used to help the students create their masterpieces, I explained, "I tell them the rules for the contest, and we brainstorm ideas about the theme. Then I simply say, 'Art it.' When I looked at the resulting work, if I thought it wasn't as good as it could be, I'd say, 'Do it better.' And they did!"*

> *Later, when Jack Toebe—lovingly referred to as 'our godfather,' and other donors (angels) began supporting the school, we hired a real art teacher. One day she hung a painting by Van Gogh on the wall for the art classes. Our children had become so accustomed to the excellent art created by their peers that a child walked in, saw the print, and exclaimed, "Dang, that's good! Which kid did it?"*

One year the city of Philadelphia held a competition titled "Listen Up: Kids Have Something to Say about Domestic Violence." As usual, Sister Jeannette asked the children to "Art it," which for this contest could include the creation of poems and essays, as well as visual art.

A boy from Sierra Leone turned in a picture of his village back home: planes were dropping bombs, people on the ground had weapons, and children were hiding under trees. When Sister Jeannette asked him about his drawing, he said that was the domestic violence he knew. Mayor Ed Rendell presented the awards at City

Hall. Although the Sierra Leonean child was not among them, St. Francis students took home six of the eight honors for art and three of the eight for essays. Our children, many of whom had suffered immeasurable losses, learned the power of hope and optimism and good preparation.

Sister Jeannette:

> *Not everything contest-wise was positive. Indeed, we discovered something very sad as a result of that Domestic Violence competition. As I read the 30 or 40 entries, two stood out. The two were sisters. One wrote an essay, the other a poem, and both pieces were upsetting—and too realistic to be fiction.*
>
> *We notified child welfare personnel and from the investigation learned that an uncle was abusing both girls. I asked, "Is your bedroom door locked?" "No," was the reply. "He took the doors off our rooms."*
>
> *That was just another reminder of many over the years that as our kids sat in front of us in their school uniforms, desperate family situations could be hidden inside.*
>
> *The following was one of the entries in the contest:*

Why Does the Violence Come to Me?

Why is it that when you hit me, touch me, scream at me,

    I feel that the whole world hates me.

Why is it that when you're drunk, you come to me for pleasure,

    to solve your problems.

Why is it that the finger is always pointed at me when something

    goes wrong, and the one who needs pointing at is you.

I remember that night when you did what you did to me, you begged

    for my forgiveness and a promise not to tell anyone.

And the other time when I was asleep, I felt you on me and the only

    thing I did right was to tell you to stop.

That night in my sleep I cried and prayed to God an 'Our Father'

    to forgive you for your sins and for trespassing me.

I never thought I'd be the one to have to go through mental abuse

    as others have – all I wanted to do was to be different from that.

I call it mental abuse because I always cry and put myself down now,

    because I feel that no one loves me, because of what you did to me.

And still I don't know

Why the Violence Comes to Me . . .

ENCOURAGING TALENT

The empty classroom we used for art was full of 'stuff,' odds and ends that Sister Jeannette had saved thinking it might be useful—and it was; the kids used it all. They had to be creative because we didn't have authentic art supplies. Once we needed an 'ugly' tree for a school assembly, and students made a truly ugly one out of used stockings and panty hose, and another out of steel wool pads.

Kitakiya, a short, slight young girl from Jamaica nicknamed Kitty, had remarkable artistic talent. Fresh-faced, with coffee-toned skin, she wore her hair tightly braided, straight back, and her eyes were always darting around, noticing everything. Recognizing her talent, we applied for—and she received—a very competitive Marian Anderson Award for Young Artists. The award paid for all the art materials she needed to set up her own studio at home.

Sister Jeannette:

> *Kitty and I worked a whole weekend putting together a list from a huge art catalogue. There was no heat in the school on weekends, so we put space heaters in a little office where we worked. I still remember her sitting with her coat on, shivering with a mixture of cold and excitement as she picked out art supplies and told me what she would do with them.*
>
> *At first, she pointed to small items like a packet of eight pastels, overlooking the packets of 16 and 32. I encouraged her to think about what she really wished for, and I could see her eyes widen as she began to dream bigger dreams. As we looked at page after page, she could barely breathe, gasping "Wow" and "Oh," not quite able to believe that it was possible for her to have such a large assortment of*

brushes, canvases, and paints.

After Kitty moved on from St. Francis to high school with her new supplies, we asked her to paint a beach scene that we could present to Jeannie and Mike O'Neill, the donor angels who had built the school's new Art and Music Center. Since Kitty had never been to the seashore, we showed her photos of a lighthouse, dunes with reeds, and the ocean and told her that the name of the family's home on the Jersey shore was "Summer Wind."

Sometime later, Kitty returned with a pencil sketch for our approval before she committed it to oils. Her work, as always, was exceptional, but we couldn't figure out what was flying in the air; it didn't look like seagulls. "What is all of this?" I asked.

"That's trash blowing all over the beach. You said to make it a summer windy day." I explained to her that unlike some of our local neighborhoods, there was probably no trash on the beach near the O'Neill summer home—and that a few seagulls would fit the bill.

The final painting was exquisite! When they heard the story, Jeannie and Mike O'Neill said they wished we had saved Kitty's original sketch.

A WIDE RANGE OF TALENT—AND AWARDS

There were annual art and essay contests about Philadelphia's Fairmount Park, one of the largest urban green spaces in the United States. Our students lived far away from the park, but once we researched and talked about its wonders, they penned and painted marvelous renditions from their imaginations. The result: seven Aristocrat Flowering Pear trees over seven years awarded for first place. They were planted with great ceremony and lined the street in front of the school.

In a children's map competition, two St. Francis eighth graders' works were named United States finalists for the International Cartographic Conference in Barcelona, Spain! (They were not, however, summoned to Spain.) In 1997, the school—a Catholic school, mind you—won two of the top prizes in a poster contest celebrating the 50th Anniversary of the State of Israel!

One of our more remarkable victories came when a St. Francis student won the Delaware Valley Chemistry Society poster contest sponsored by the American Chemistry Society. His poster was displayed in buses and trolleys all over the city with his name and school. And we didn't even teach chemistry!

A SPECIAL FAMILY

The Tran Family, newly arrived from Vietnam, included five girls who attended St. Francis. The oldest graduated the year before we came. Her father was unable to attend her graduation ceremony because he couldn't get time off from his job as a housepainter.

At the very time the ceremony was taking place, he touched an aluminum ladder to a hot electric wire and was electrocuted— leaving his wife, who knew almost no English, to raise their six young children alone in a strange land.

As Sister Jeannette discovered, all the daughters were artists, and their work was soon entered in just about every art contest in the city and surrounding areas. With deep black hair cut in bangs across her forehead, each sister was like a carbon copy of the others, just a little bigger or smaller. All were slight, quick, smart, precise, gentle, sometimes sad, though able to smile and giggle—and very talented.

Whatever the contest, they always won, and their prizes contributed to their St. Francis tuition and helped the family survive. Over the years, the Tran sisters received awards from four Pennsylvania governors: Dick Thornburgh, Bob Casey, Tom Ridge, and Mark Schweiker.

So Much More Than Artists!

The four Tran sisters who graduated from de Sales during our years at the school went on to great academic success:

Linh (1985 graduate)

BA Architecture, University of Pennsylvania

MA Architecture, Yale

Huyen (1987)

BFA, University of Pennsylvania

MFA, Tyler School of Art

Phoi (1992)

BS Plant Science, Cornell

PhD, University of California, Berkeley

Trinh (1993)

BA Sociology, University of Chicago

PhD, University of California, Berkeley

"EVERYBODY CAN BE GOOD AT SOMETHING"

The school's success in contests did not just improve our community's confidence and morale. While the activities themselves were competitive, they had the effect of encouraging students to see beyond themselves and be supportive of one another. The children began to see themselves not just as they were, but what they could be.

Sister Constance:

> *One year, five or six of our students took the very competitive test to be a Neumann Scholar—a scholarship program to help academically talented eighth graders attend an Archdiocesan high school. Only one of the students was successful. (For us that was unusual since we often had two or three a year.) When the solitary winner was announced at a school assembly, the entire class clapped enthusiastically for her. Mrs. Riley, representing the Connelly Foundation which awards the Neumann scholarships, asked if any students could share some insights about the winner.*

> *Immediately hands shot up, including those of several young people who had competed for the same scholarship and had just learned the disappointing results for themselves. This generous spirit impressed Mrs. Riley and she complimented the students in the group.*

Sister Jeannette:

> *Two quotes from St. Francis kids have stuck with me: One came from Lucille, a young girl with big eyes, moving parts absolutely everywhere, and a squeaky*

high-pitched voice. "God," she once wrote, "has given us so much talent, and we do our best to use it."

The second requires a little background. We had a quiet, introverted boy who had learning challenges and, we realized, needed special placement. But his parents would not hear of it. They said he had made more progress at St. Francis than they had ever imagined possible. We actually had them sign a document stating we had informed them of his special needs but that they'd chosen to keep him at St. Francis anyway.

One day, a visitor to the seventh-grade classroom asked what made St. Francis de Sales School special. We were shocked when this young lad raised his hand to answer. "The thing that makes this school so great," he said, "is that there are so many things to do that everybody can be good at something." That says it all.

A GRADUATE LOOKS BACK:

Kyrus L. Freeman '91

Kyrus L. Freeman, 38, is a graduate of the University of Pennsylvania and Vanderbilt Law School. He is a partner in the Washington, D.C., office of Holland & Knight LLP where he focuses on land use, zoning, and municipal law. He lives in suburban Maryland.

I started at St. Francis de Sales in fourth grade and attended through eighth. I wasn't Catholic, but I remember the full page newspaper ads and 60-second radio spots run by the Philly Archdiocese at the time: "A Catholic School Education. You'll Value the Values." My folks valued the values of a Catholic education.

Sister Constance was always nice and had a quiet manner. Sister Jeannette is the best teacher I ever had, and I've had some good teachers. She made me realize that nuns are people—that they have other interests and lives outside of the convent.

I remember having to recite the names of the presidents. Sister Jeannette was very focused on making sure we learned the subject matter. I participated in a lot of contests. My mom has pictures of me standing next to art projects. De Sales treats art and creativity as important parts of education. The contests encouraged us to reach higher. Looking back, I think de Sales provided the necessary foundation to go out and do well at the next levels of life. The school had academic rigor and gave me the foundation to think.

It was a diverse school. One of my very best friends, Thanh, is Vietnamese. We met at de Sales, and he was the best man at my wedding. I do not recall any racial issues. There was so much diversity—racially, culturally, and even physically. We had blind students from St. Lucy, and de Sales students had to help them navigate the building. It was a nurturing environment.

Poverty was not something I was conscious of growing up. School uniforms take away the sense of who has what. Why does SFDS work as well as it does? There are two constants: Sister C and Sister J. They care about the students and the school. All schools have an academic model they adhere to, but people make the difference.

I don't think that I would be where I am today if I hadn't gone to SFDS—had I not experienced those constants. They set the foundation for the next trajectory. It is amazing how much they did with so little. They filled the gaps with their commitment to the students, and what they achieved is miraculous.

CHAPTER FOUR

Kids Can Do Anything: The Speech Tournament

The ability to speak in public is an important skill that can give anyone—and certainly a child—greater confidence. That's why the annual Metropolitan Philadelphia Speech Tournament was the premier event on our competition calendar.

Each year in preparation for this inter-school contest, eighth-graders prepared a few lines and auditioned for one of our school's 10 to 15 slots across the designated categories such as declamation, original composition, and oral interpretation of prose and poetry.

We picked the students who had the most potential, and the children not chosen became their coaches. That way the entire class worked together to get ready for the tournament—and rejoiced together when we won trophies, which we did every year.

Developing these winners involved so much.

Proper pronunciation. We were working with children who had their own special pronunciations. It sometimes seemed that the "th" sound had completely disappeared from the English language. Every year we had to change *wiff to with, teef to teeth, birffday to birthday*, and *dis to this*.

Sister Jeannette, who single-handedly prepped our contestants, cut out 36-inch signs with the correct pronunciations and put them all around the classroom. The word 'to' was another challenge; it often came out as ta. So, she went through the students' readings and replaced every 'to' with the number 2. And on occasion she employed still another learning aid.

Sister Jeannette:

> *The kids could expect a chalk eraser to come tossed at them if they forgot the correct pronunciation—that is, once we got to know each other. Actually, they seemed to enjoy the eraser exercise and sometimes misspoke for fun to see if I was <u>really</u> listening.*
>
> *Pronunciation practice helped not only the children preparing to give a speech, but also the whole class.*

<u>Meaning and interpretation</u>. Many of the readings were challenging, and before beginning to work on the lines, Sister Jeannette would explain the background of the piece and its message.

Edgar Allan Poe's poem "The Bells", for example, is a very difficult piece, yet one that over the years proved highly successful for the school. Poe hears so much in the ringing of the bells: from the youthful experience of first love—'Silver bells! What a world of merriment their melody foretells' to death—'Iron bells! What a world of solemn thought their monody compels.'

Sister Jeannette:

> *I would recite a few lines of the poem, doing my best to express the meaning, and then tell the coaches they had to get that same result. When the coaches felt their charges had the first few lines down, they would come back, and I would give them a few more*

to learn.

Remember, there were as many as 15 kids and 15 coaches. Before classes began each day, I could hear them all practicing in various rooms and stairwells. As the years went by, I knew all the selections by heart. If I overheard a recitation that was incorrect or not powerful enough, I would run out and correct the coach as well as the orator.

Memorization. We had the students memorize and practice their pieces line-by-line. A big reason for this incremental approach was that once a child memorizes something incorrectly, it is nearly impossible to unlearn it.

One eighth grader, William, proudly announced that over the previous summer he had learned Walt Whitman's "O Captain! My Captain!" But it was immediately obvious that he had not fully grasped the message behind the words, and he was never able to make it sound right. Much to his disappointment, he didn't make the tournament team.

(William, however, did not let that setback stop him. He went on to Howard University, where he was president of the College of Arts and Sciences student council and earned bachelor's and law degrees. He now practices in Washington, D.C.)

Eye contact. It was difficult for many of our children to learn to make eye contact. Sister Jeannette encouraged them to pretend that the classroom's empty desks were filled with people—to prepare them for an audience of judges, other contestants, and parents on tournament day. It was crucial they not simply stare at one spot.

Sister Jeannette:

Having the children recognize the judges was very

important. "They will be the ones with stopwatches, clipboards, and papers," I would tell the students. "You each know the strongest parts of your pieces, and that's when you make sure to look at those judges."

<u>Carrying on through distractions</u>. During much of their practice, Sister Jeannette had the students shout their lines. That got them used to hearing themselves speak and helped prepare them to continue on through interruptions.

The tournament venue rotated among area schools and colleges—institutions that typically used bells to signal the start and end of classes. At some competitions, we had seen students freeze at a ringing bell, but not our kids.

Sister Jeannette:

> *Sending the young orators to other classrooms in our school to present their pieces was also helpful. You can imagine a roomful of second graders giggling during a moving rendition of "To the tintinnabulation that so musically wells From the bells, bells, bells, bells, bells, bells, bells." After that, nothing can faze our contestants on tournament day.*

<u>Preparation schedule</u>. Because the preparation was so intense, we didn't start working with the students until three weeks before the tournament. When teachers at other schools heard that, they couldn't believe it. Three weeks? At those schools, preparations continued throughout the whole year. But we knew we couldn't hold the kids' interest that long—or ours, either.

Each day leading up to the tournament, the speakers and their coaches would arrive at school at 7:15 a.m. and practice in the fire stairways at the ends of the hallways. The coaches made sure their contestants shouted a few lines at a time. The many young voices echoed off the brick walls and concrete stairs. I listened and told each team when their initial lines sounded good enough to go on to the next ones. We repeated the routine at lunchtime and again after school.

On the day before the tournament, the contestants, accompanied by their coaches, went around to all the classrooms and recited their pieces. It was a tradition—a day the orators had dreamed of since listening to their predecessors in previous years. After each presentation, the speaker and coach would ask the teacher and students for a critique, and often got helpful ones.

Through all of this, the coaches played a critical role. They became stakeholders in the outcome and could be tougher on the orators than Sister Jeannette—and that's hard!

Sister Jeannette:

> *We reminded the students that when you watch the Olympics on TV, you see that as soon as an athlete finishes performing, he or she stands beside the coach. And it's the coach who receives the first hug when the scores are announced. These athletes know well that it is their coach who got them to the Olympics, and so the coach shares in the moment.*

> *Unfortunately, our coaches couldn't literally share in the moment. Because of limited transportation space, we weren't able to take them to the tournament. So they had to stay behind and wait impatiently for a phone call reporting the results.*

Sister Jeannette: A Recollection

When a student won at the speech tournament, we recorded his or her presentation so kids in subsequent years could take the recording home at night and practice.

A student I will call Adesoye (not her real name) was fabulous with Poe's "The Bells" and took first place. Her facial muscles hardly moved, but her eyes seemed to get larger as she gave voice to each bell.

A few years later when Adesoye was in high school, I telephoned to ask if she would make a new video of her rendition of "The Bells." Our tapes had been ruined in a horrific school fire (a Sunday afternoon in 2000 when Sister Constance and Sister Jeannette were the only ones in the building), and we needed a new tape of Poe's poem for a student wanting to do the piece.

Adesoye laughed brightly at hearing my voice and immediately agreed. I told her I would pick her up the following Saturday morning and return her home when we finished the taping.

On Saturday, I drove to her home but didn't beep, thanks be to God, as I learned later. I just waited. Finally, she came out and down the steps. I sensed something wrong, strange, different about the way she carried herself.

She got in the car, and when I turned to greet her, I saw her lip was cut and swollen and her left eye horribly bruised and partly shut. She didn't say anything. I quickly drove off but a block away pulled over and said, "Tell me... Your father?"

"Yes. Again."

My heart broke. Adesoye was so strong, so giving, so willing to help me, and I can still see her father in my mind—a giant of a man with a harsh and intimidating voice. Adesoye told me her school counselor was taking care of the situation.

Needless to say, we didn't shoot a <u>video</u> that day. Adesoye recorded an audiocassette instead, and we chatted about her future plans to attend college and earn a nursing degree "so I can help people."

Post script: She did go on to earn that degree, and now her own beautiful little daughter attends St. Francis de Sales.

TOURNAMENT DAY: Butterflies and the Burbs

The morning of the Metropolitan Speech Tournament, the contestants stand around the school auditorium facing the wall and shouting their pieces as loudly as they can. They need to get the sleep out of their voices. As we drive to the tournament site in the school van, Sister Jeannette tells them to continue reciting out loud—it helps keep the butterflies at bay.

The ride to the burbs is itself strange enough. The experience of going outside the city is unique for many of the students. On a trip to Bishop McDevitt High School northwest of Philadelphia near Wyncote, they're excited by all of the 'Leave It to Beaver' houses they see. Another year, on the way to Cardinal O'Hara High west of Philadelphia in Delaware County, a student comments, "These people in the suburbs are really rich, aren't they, Sister?"

"Why do you say that?"

"Look at all the oxygen they have from grass and trees!"

In the van on the way we talk about what to expect and how to behave, remind the students to shake hands, to speak loudly enough to be heard, and to look each person in the eye.

Sister Jeannette:

Of course, I could never do anything about the fact that at every tournament for 20 years, our students were practically the only minority kids there. I instructed them to go out of their way to speak to kids from all the other schools—to try to make conversation, ask what schools they represent, and so on.

Yet each year, it felt like a hard smack as I watched them react to the hundreds of mostly white kids crowded into the registration space. Some of our contestants obviously felt out of place, if not unwelcomed. At the end of the day, however, our students experienced an emotion 100 percent positive—when members of our team were called repeatedly to the stage to pick up trophies.

One year when we arrived at a local college for the tournament, I took our kids into an empty classroom for a final briefing. An adult I didn't know came in and began chatting and asked the name of our school.

When the students answered, the man said, "Didn't I see you on TV last week?" Indeed, the school's Peace Program [described in Chapter 5] had been featured on local television the week before. "You're famous for sports, aren't you?" the gentleman inquired.

To which a girl proudly responded, "No, sir. We're famous for education!"

I wanted to scream, "Black kids are good at a lot more than sports, mister!" A little later when he gave the welcome talk, we discovered our visitor was the president of the college. At that tournament, St. Francis won more trophies than any other school. "The proof is in the pudding."

St. Francis de Sales Sweeps Tournament

3/25/96 Used with permission Southwest Globe

Another year the competition drew 19 schools from across the five-county area. Before the scoring, a forensics coach from one of the other schools told us about another tournament that we might want to enter. After we won four first-place trophies and one finalist certificate, the coach said with a laugh <u>that perhaps we shouldn't enter after all!</u>

DeSales wins West Catholic Speech Tournament for eighth year in a row

4/23/98 Used with permission Southwest Globe

On one occasion, a student won the first-place certificate and trophy for declamation with Patrick Henry's "Give Me Liberty" speech. When we arrived at his house, he said thanks for the ride and jumped out of the van.

I called after him, "Jason, you forgot your trophy and certificate. Take them so you can show your family."

"No, that's okay, Sister. Just leave them at school, and I'll show my coach on Monday." Jason KNEW his coach would be proud. (I wondered if anyone at home would be interested...)

IT ALL WORKED OUT: One Tournament We Won't Forget

It was Tournament Saturday. The plan was for the contestants to gather at school at 7 a.m. and leave for the venue by 7:30. But 7:30 arrived, and Lola had not; 7:40 and still no Lola. Panic.

Sister Jeannette scurried to the school office, looked up Lola's home phone number, and called. Lola answered and through tears said her mom wouldn't let her come. We knew Lola's home life was rocky, and Sister Jeannette suppressed the urge to be harsh. Instead, she gave assurances it would all work out, hung up, and phoned Lola's coach.

"Please, can I talk to Yirgalem?"

"She's asleep," replied the little voice on the other end. Yirgalem had four or five brothers and sisters in our school, and the voice had to belong to one of them.

"Please tell her to wake up and talk to me. It's her teacher." The word teacher was certain to get her out of bed. The next voice was Yirgalem.

"Yirgalem, Lola can't come to the speech tournament. Sister Constance will pick you up in 15 minutes, and I'll bring your piece for you. Hurry!"

Thank God her home was not far off the route to the venue. Sister Constance drove in the convent car, and Sister Jeannette took the rest of the team in the school's old, beat-up van.

There was a collective sigh of relief along with a few quiet cheers as Sister Constance and Yirgalem appeared in the tournament registration room where the St. Francis team was waiting. Sister Constance took over the registration process, and Sister Jeannette turned her attention to the former-coach-now-contestant standing dazed before her.

"Sister, I can't do this. I forget how it goes."

"No need to worry. I have the piece right here with the markings that you and Lola put on it as you practiced."

Yirgalem looked still half asleep, and we couldn't help but notice that she had slept on her cornrows; they were not as tight and perfect as usual. Sister Jeannette took her to the far end of the building to help her practice the presentation: "No Boy... I'm a GIRL!" It is the story of a young girl who organizes a protest against a rule that forbade boys to wear blue jeans in a high school.

Starting off, Yirgalem's voice caught, and her delivery was a bit iffy. But as she went along, she grew firmer and more convincing, and before she came to the end, it happened: the coach gave way to the orator.

Later in front of the judges, Yirgalem was as strong as we could have hoped for. When they awarded her second place, she was so shocked and thrilled, she almost melted. The rest of the team was just as elated and awarded her high fives all around.

THE KEY

Kids can do anything, not if, but when you believe in them, encourage them, provide them with a safe place to do whatever their "thing" is, prepare them for the right way to act in every circumstance, AND CELEBRATE EVERYTHING.

At St. Francis de Sales we had the philosophy that there are no individual winners—we're all in this together. Every kid's win is a success for their coaches, their peers, and for the whole school. And that's not just for speech contests. It's for everything they do. <u>WE</u> know these kids can be great. Our challenge is to make sure <u>THEY</u> know it, too!

Being positive with the students about what they could do was so important. At school assemblies we often sang the song "I Am a Promise" by Bill and Gloria Gaither:

> I am a promise,
>
> I am a possibility
>
> I am a promise with a capital P;
>
> I can be anything, anything God wants me to be.
>
>
> You are a promise!
>
> You are a possibility!
>
> You are a promise with a capital P;
>
> You are a great big bundle of potentiality.

Sister Jeannette:

> *Let me tell you about an African American student I will call Loren. He came to St. Francis after his first Catholic school closed when he was in the seventh grade. Entering a new school is always difficult, and at first I thought that was his only challenge.*

But as time went on, other issues became evident. He had difficulty learning, participating, and making friends in class and on the playground. I can still see him: bored, tired, sometimes almost defiant, his head down on the desk, completely absent.

When tournament time came around, he did not join in the tryouts. I asked him to stay after school and told him that I had come across a speech that seemed just right for him. He shook his head and said no, he didn't want to do it.

"Just listen to me. There's an amazing story behind this speech—Frederick Douglass's 'What to the Slave is the Fourth of July?' This famous escaped slave had been invited to give a speech in Rochester, New York, on July 4th in 1852. The speech he gave, however, was not at all what the crowd expected."

I stood and delivered some of the lines: 'Fellow Citizens: Pardon me, and allow me to ask, why am I called to speak here today? What have I, or those I represent, to do with your national independence? Are the great principles of freedom and justice, embodied in that Declaration of Independence, extended to us?'

"Loren," I explained, "Douglass went on to tell the crowd that although they were celebrating freedom, there were many thousands who could not." Loren sat for a while staring and then said quietly, "Yes, I'll do that... if you'll help me."

We worked for hours in secret. He was unwilling to practice when others were around. I will never forget the day that I called his name at lunchtime to deliver his speech before the rest of the class. I don't know what was more powerful—his rendering or his classmates' astonishment!

Everything changed that day for Loren. He truly got inside Frederick Douglass's head and heart. I pondered how Loren, too, might have been held captive. The power with which he interpreted that speech took away the breath of anyone who heard him. When he spoke, it was with a different consciousness. Loren wasn't standing there in front of us; he was in Rochester, New York, and the date was July 4, 1852.

Loren won a first-place trophy. Yet more importantly, he also won the respect and admiration of his classmates and a new appreciation for himself. It showed in the way he talked and carried himself. And significantly for me, how he looked others in the eye.

But the story didn't end there. Over the next four years, Loren took trolleys and buses from his high school to de Sales to coach students who chose the Douglass speech—and he made winners out of every one of them!

IT'S NOT JUST ABOUT TROPHIES

We usually had winners in the competitions we entered, but there were, of course, St. Francis contestants who did not win. We knew how important it was for them to accept and learn from the results.

We worked to make sure all the children recognized when they had done their best. Kids know—we all know—when we've done something worthwhile. And that knowledge was a prize they earned, treasured, and deserved, whatever the outcome.

There can be so much hidden talent. Sometimes we were shocked at what our students produced—pure natural ability just waiting to pop out.

We had a boy just two years out of a refugee camp who never stopped moving, tapping, bouncing around; Sister Jeannette considered him a poster boy for ADHD. One afternoon, she wanted to talk to him after class. Because a few other kids had questions for her, she told the young man, "Just wait at your desk and write something."

"What should I write?"
"Write a poem."
"What's a poem?"

"Put your thoughts into words ...and they don't have to rhyme."

The following is an unrevised copy of what the child handed in 20 minutes later:

N I G H T : A Teenager's View

I walk slowly on soft grass
I stop to sit on a bench
Nature gently invites me to its evening celebration.

The cool autumn breezes caress my face and
soothe my body after a hard day.
I put my hands in my pockets and enjoy the night.
I forget the problems of the day.

Now I can hear freely.
I listen to crickets chirping twilight songs.
They invite me to sing with them.

I gaze at the sky as the black curtain unrolls.
The stars show off shy twinkles, dancing gracefully in the heavens.
They call on me to join their dance.

Some believe that night is one of fear's weapons.

But I think it is a pleasure promised by nature
For restless teenagers seeking the freedom of adults.

Our message is that every kid can excel at something. It is extraordinary to watch students begin to think: We can be somebody. First, it's "We" at St. Francis de Sales can be somebody. But then that turns into "I" can be somebody. You can almost see it in their faces as this mindset takes over. Their whole stance expresses newfound promise and possibility. A visitor one day said, "Your children all walk with their heads up and with confidence."

We have experienced the miracles that working with kids this way can achieve. We also believe that this approach has enormous value far beyond the walls of St. Francis de Sales. We suspect there are millions of Americans—kids, teachers, parents, people of every age—who need someone to inspire them to do better by believing that they can do better and encouraging them along the way.

A group of eager St. Francis de Sales second grade students brimming with possibility... potentiality!

A GRADUATE LOOKS BACK:

Rashana Barnes-Miller '94

Rashana, 35, has a degree in letters, arts, and sciences at Penn State and a Master's in urban studies at Eastern University. At Penn State she starred in basketball, earning All-Big Ten honors her junior and senior years. She was selected in the 3rd round of the 2002 Women's National Basketball Association by the Los Angeles Sparks. She has had assistant coaching positions at St. Joseph's, Loyola Chicago, and Rider universities, and for three years was the basketball coach and then assistant principal at her alma mater, West Catholic Prep in Philadelphia. Rashana and her husband, John Miller, now live in Richmond, Virginia, with their recently adopted son.

—

I began at St. Francis de Sales in kindergarten. I think it was natural that I would go there. My mother and aunt went there and so did my older and younger sibs. I'm a lifer. I met my best friend, April, at the beginning of fourth grade, and she was matron of honor at my wedding.

A great memory of mine was that our eighth-grade class held a conference to promote using public transportation. So many kids had asthma, and we wanted to do something about it. SEPTA is our regional public transit authority, and we convinced them to give free rides for one day in an effort to get people out of their cars. I wrote the theme song: "Ride Septa, Ride Septa today. Save lots of money on Try

Transit Thursday." It was played for days on KYW Radio. I remember a television crew was there. That was BIG! Later I learned that many of the ideas we proposed were adopted for public transit.

Sister Jeannette was very businesslike. Something she said stuck with me: "You know, there will never be a woman president because women complain about their cramps too much." Of course, she didn't mean it seriously, but to this day, I think about that before I complain. Sister Jeannette lost part of a finger in an accident in Alaska, but she always said, "I'm alive. I'm good." Who's going to complain to a nun waving half a finger at you!

I remember days when Sister Constance would announce our basketball scores on the PA system, and I would be puffing up my chest. Sister Jeannette never looked too impressed. She would tell me, "You are more than basketball. Don't let anyone put you in that box." She always wanted us to Think Bigger and Be Bigger. We lived in a world of possibilities. It was just a limitless environment. That sentiment helped me to move away from coaching. I returned to school to get a Master's in urban studies.

Although Sister Constance was tough, she was very calming. She didn't have to yell; her presence commanded respect. She was watching the day I tried out for sixth-grade basketball, and she thought I was so good that she got me a scholarship to a summer basketball camp. This was a big deal for me and set me on a path of success. I was impressed—a nun who knew basketball!

I remember kids from all over—a lot of Vietnamese,

Eritreans, Ethiopians—and they didn't seem different. They were just other people. We all played together. We were all friends and hung out together. From kindergarten through eighth, that was our world; that was our normal. It builds so much tolerance.

St. Francis de Sales was a loving place yet always kept its standards. I think some people don't expect enough of African American kids. When they're doing well, many assume that's the best they can do. But at de Sales, they don't congratulate you for doing what you <u>should</u> be doing. It was just a known fact that they hold you to an even higher standard.

St. Francis de Sales is the house that Sister Constance and Sister Jeannette built. Everybody there is an extension of them and their vision. They have a standard, and they refuse to let kids get away with stuff. Their method is tried and true. They have a way of building a child's moral compass, and they're not straying from it. I love that.

CHAPTER FIVE

Blessed Are the Peacemakers

Sister Constance:

One day Sister Jeannette rushed into the convent sobbing her heart out. It took several minutes before I could get her to tell me what was wrong.

While driving our wonderful convent cook to her home farther along in Southwest Philly, Sister Jeannette slowed the car at a stop sign, and a teenager crossing the street was shot to death right in front of them. Paralyzed with shock and fear, the two could only watch as the shooter ran right past their car and into an alley. Somehow, Sister Jeannette pulled herself together enough to take the woman home and return to the convent.

After a long silence, Sister told me that she now understood how one of her students felt two weeks earlier when he was very upset all day. He told her he had seen someone shot in front of his home the day before. She had tried to console him, but Calvin said that nothing would erase the memory. Now Sister Jeannette knew that to be true for herself as well.

Violence surrounded our school—and was for so many of our students an intimate part of their young lives. Second grader Jose was proud to show us that he could read. Looking at the Prayer Wall (a bulletin board for the names of all who asked for prayers), he pointed to the funeral card of a recently deceased grad. "I know what that RIP (said in word form to rhyme with 'tip') means," indicating the letters after the man's name. "RIP means somebody got shot." Our friend had died of natural causes, but sadly, our little one didn't know any other RIP! The piles of Teddy bears, balloons and RIP signs that appear in our neighborhood so often are what Jose knows. Neither 'Rest in Peace' nor 'Requiescat in Pace' was part of his experience.

One day during fourth-grade class, some of the children suddenly dove under their desks shouting, "Bullets, get down!" "Don't be silly," said the teacher. "That's a car backfiring." Little did we know until after school that there had been a shooting rampage outside. The proof was in the bullet casings lying all over the street. Those fourth graders knew what they were talking about.

Eighth graders talked at lunch time about the nine-year-old boy who was shot in our local Kingsessing playground. "It was his own fault he got shot. Everybody knows you have to check out who's already there or who's driving around before you go in to play at Kingsessing. It's his own fault he got shot!"

Once a year, a second-grade teacher told her class to write a letter to someone they loved. "Aniah," age 7, wrote to her mother:

Great Job!

Dear Mom I love you so much
I wish you will come back because I had so much fun when you were here.
Good for You!
Your Pal, A

"Dear Mom, I love you so much. I wish you will come back because I had so much fun when you were here. Your pal Aniah." (Aniah was never told that the decomposed body of her mother had been found in an abandoned drug house.)

Dec. 12-15-06

Dear Jesus,
I hope your taking care of my friend Isiah and my Uncle in heaven. I miss Isiah and my Uncle very much. Tell Isiah that evrybody misses him very much!
Love, R
7 years old
(he got Shot when he was in his car)

Here's another child's Christmas letter.

Note the P.S. ("he got shot when he was in his car")

The following were displayed outside the fourth-grade classroom on Dr. King's birthday. They are not your typical "I Have a Dream" responses from nine-year-olds.

I have a dream...

It will not be any
more shoteing. So I will not be scared to go
outside. Or open the door. And to not be scared to
go to sleep at night. And that is my dream

That I won't have
to be scared to go to my window at
night.

that all the fighting
will stop. That I don't have to hear gun
shot up the street, down street or on my
block.

that people could go
to the store with out being scared of getting
shot or at home getting robbed

Jamas entendemos el porque de tu partida pero, nos satisface saber que te fuiste como viniste, en paz.

Lina M. Sanchez
Noviembre 30, 1962

Juana L. Nuñez
Enero 27, 1967

Porfirio A. Nuñez
Octubre 17, 1961

Septiembre 6, 2011

In a three-year span, one of our city's two newspapers, *The Philadelphia Daily News*, reported on four violent robberies/deaths involving St. Francis de Sales families:

A Southwest Philadelphia store owner was fatally shot in front of his wife by a robber (September 2009). The couple's son and daughter were our children, and Monsignor Walsh wanted us to come with him when he told the children about their father.

The owner of a West Philadelphia grocery was closing for the day when he, his wife, and sister were shot to death; the gunmen fled (September 2011). The victims' nieces and nephews attended St. Francis. Then the orphaned son came to us as well. Sister Constance noticed that he hadn't put information about his now-deceased parents on the application. She quietly told him, "You may not have a phone number for them or an address, but they will ALWAYS be your parents." Attending that funeral with the three caskets in the front of church and the inconsolable elderly parents of the dad and aunt left an indelible imprint on our hearts.

A West Philadelphia man was handcuffed, threatened with a machete, and robbed in a home invasion witnessed by his two daughters (August 2012). The daughters were St. Francis students. They had unlocked the door thinking it was their dad coming home from work.

An attempted armed robbery of a West Philadelphia market failed, and the storeowner chased and opened fire on the fleeing robber. "I do what I had to do," the owner was quoted as saying (October 2012). He had four children in our school. They had, thankfully, not been left orphaned.

Sister Constance:

> *When I was little and came into the house to tell my mother about an affront I had received while playing, my mother would always say, "Fight your own battles." She never got involved in the spats among neighborhood children.*
>
> *Today, we cannot tell children to fight their own battles; now there are pit bulls, baseball bats, razors, knives, and guns. Today, spats can turn into homicides.*
>
> *Too many of our young boys grew up to be wounded or killed in drive-by shootings and drug-related assassinations. Twelve young men who attended St. Francis de Sales during our years there have since been murdered—twelve that we know of, that is.*
>
> *Violence has reached into my own family, too. My grandniece, Claire, who attended our school for*

five years, chose to become a teacher after college. In 2003, she was brutally murdered, and her body set on fire in Philadelphia's Fairmount Park. All the funerals that we had attended did not prepare me for this personal loss.

A recent graduate had been suspended from his high school for unpaid tuition and couldn't go back for two days. He had been home alone all day and was sitting on his front steps. Suddenly, he became a witness to a shooting in front of his house. He bolted away and ended up at de Sales asking Sister Constance if he could talk to her about it in the Peace Room. Sister did her best to console Paul and told him he should come back to help us for the next two days.

Later that week, the story was in the local newpaper. Recognizing that the graphic photo would upset readers, the editor wrote, "We hope this makes you sick. We also hope this picture spurs you to do something about the violence…"

WESTSIDE WEEKLY   September 17 - 23, 2010

Our Streets Running Red

By Tyree Johnson
Editor/Publisher

Some people will be very upset with the Westside Weekly for running this very graphic picture of a dead Rasul Rahman Gresham.

In fact, many will aim their anger at this newspaper rather than the youngsters who created this horrible scene.

But we wanted our readers, our neighbors in this community, to see up close the effects of the breakdown of the moral fiber in some of our youthful residents.

We hope this makes you sick.

We also hope this picture

He was no angel, according to interviews by neighbors who knew him.

But he was the middle child of Ansonia Gresham, the matriarch of a family that has seen its share of trouble.

She received the news of her son's murder by neighbors banging on her door around 11 Thursday morning.

"One woman was screaming 'Tell her! Tell her!" to a man who was crying uncontrollably, she recalled. "Tell me what!" I shouted. "Rasul is dead!" the man replied.

"That took a bit of my soul," she said. "Here was

An officer gathers evidence near the body of a murdered Rasul Gresham

told the Westside Weekly that   him to seek peace and to   turns."

9/17/2010 Used with permission Westside Weekly

PEACE PROGRAM: The First Step

By 1993, we had been at the school for eight years and had attended too many funerals for murder victims and consoled too many grieving parents and children. We realized that speaking at funerals and visiting victims' homes was not enough. Though our condolences were heartfelt, we were being reactive. We had to find a way to not simply provide support to those in mourning, but to help prevent violence.

From that realization evolved our Peace Program. The first step was the Peace Wall. We brainstormed and came up with the idea of setting aside a prominent school wall where we would hang photos of children who stuck their necks out as peacemakers—children with the courage not to fight.

We wanted to reward children for behavior that contributed to peace in the school and also outside it. We asked the teachers to identify the qualities of a peacemaker and encouraged them to be on the lookout for students who exhibited those traits: intervening in a disagreement or fight or remaining particularly peaceful under stress.

Every week teachers nominated children as Peacemakers, and Sister Constance would read their names over the public-address system. Sister Jeannette then would rush to the nominees' classrooms, take their pictures, and staple the photos to a large 16-foot long by 6-foot high bulletin board in the front entranceway for everyone to see. Now dubbed The Peace Wall, it had colorful cutouts of lions, lambs, and doves. The child selected one of the three images to which we attached his or her photo. Across the top was a banner: "Blessed are the Peacemakers."

"Blessed are the Peace Makers" Once a picture was put on the Peace Wall, it stayed the whole school year. By June the wall was covered with 200 or so photos. It was delightful to see kids stop to look at their pictures and proudly point them out to friends.

Initially, we used a Polaroid OneStep camera, which is an antique today but produced instant pictures. Sister Jeannette wrote to Polaroid to tell them how the school was using its product. A few months later, some good folks from Polaroid spent the day at school taking pictures of the Peace Wall, the Peace Room, and the children. The company also featured the Peace Wall in its 1999 Annual Report and sent two cameras and a boxload of film.

Sometimes the true story behind a nomination couldn't be told. One student, for example, became depressed, took his grandfather's gun, and told his best friend that he was going to kill himself. The friend quickly grabbed the gun and threw it down the sewer. When the friend told us what had happened, we arranged counseling for the boy and his family. The friend was nominated for the Peace Wall with only a vague explanation of the reason.

Nominees did not have to be the best-behaved students. In fact, one of our biggest challenges was getting teachers to nominate difficult students. Somebody says to a teacher, "Achim did something good today," but the teacher can't help but remember that Achim is usually causing trouble. So the teacher might think, "Let's wait and see if Achim can continue being good." We tried to remind our teachers that, oftentimes, hope was all our children had to hold on to.

There was one young lad who was always in trouble and ready to fight anyone. One day another boy urinated on his arm in the lavatory, but the usually aggressive child did not retaliate. That showed heroic self-control, and the student was nominated for the Peace Wall in hopes that this new self-restraint would become a way of life for him. Of course, that description had to be carefully crafted. A few days later, the boy's mother visited the school office and cried with joy when she saw her son's photo on the Peace Wall. He had seldom been recognized for good...

Sister Jeannette:

Many schools have a demerit system. If you're caught chewing gum three times, for example, such and such will happen to you. They're constantly on the lookout for bad behavior, and that is what they find.

We don't have such a system at St. Francis de Sales, and I think that's part of our success. We watch for the good in kids. We were never looking to put angels on the Peace Wall, but real kids who were trying to improve their own or their peers' behavior. After we started celebrating good behavior, we hardly ever had any physical fighting—well, almost hardly.

Sister Constance:

We hoped the Peace Wall recognition would begin

to change the school culture. But we also asked our-selves how we might better prevent issues among students from escalating in the first place.

The public service media campaign tagline "Friends don't let friends drive drunk" had stuck with me, and I found myself paraphrasing it: "Friends don't let friends get hurt," and "Friends don't let friends get suspended."

I repeated those two lines to the children often, and over time, I started getting anonymous notes from students warning of impending trouble: "This person is planning a fight after school," or "That group of kids will be waiting for another group after recess." Those children were seeking an alternative to fighting. Here are more of their notes:

Dear Sister,

I am not planing to get in a fight thank you for your help but every one is expecting a fight lian can you say on the speaker that there is no fight because every one is expecting it. 8th & 7th. So they won't wont lagh at me and lili. and please don't till them I wrote you this note please,

thank you,

&

God Bless you

Sister Constance

Very Very Important

(Confidential)

DEAR Sis. ConsTANCE you told ME to to COME to you ANYtiME I had A problEM with Today MARch 26,1986 HER AUNt iNsulTEd ME by CAlliNg ME A big fAt thiNg. I would liKE to havE A mitt: MEEtiNg with you As soon As possiblE

Thankyou

(ANd I hAVE A witNESS)

SECOND STEP: The Peace Room

In the next phase of the Peace Program, we set aside an area where students could discuss their differences instead of fighting over them. Initially, it was a little space outside Sister Constance's office, just a large closet really, with a small table and two kid-sized chairs crammed under it.

We informed the children that if they had a disagreement with another child and talked out the problem at the table, there would be no consequences, and we would not call their parents. The idea worked so well that we created a room just for that purpose. It became known as the Peace Room.

In the middle of the room is a round table with a painting of a lion and lamb on top. The artwork was done by a friend and benefactor, Edie Dockray. She and her son, Doug, turned the space into something very special. On the table are two little stuffed animals, a lion and a lamb. The student who is the speaker holds the lamb, and then after stating his or her perspective on the issue, hands the lamb to the other child who then gives his or her viewpoint. This practice is vital when angry children all try to tell their side first.

These solemn faces demonstrate that peacemaking isn't easy. Talking it over at the Peace Table, however, is better than trying to settle it in front of others in the school yard. (There are always plenty of tissues available!)

Cheerful swirls of green, yellow, blue, and purple paint cover one wall. Another is lined with bright bookcases filled with interesting objects from all over the world, some in keeping with the lion-and-lamb motif. A crucifix with Jesus holding out a peace dove hangs on a third wall. The words "Peace on Earth" carved out of wood, and a large picture of Noah's Ark are among the other adornments.

The Peace Room is available to students all day long, and they can stay until they feel they have resolved their differences. Often they find their disagreement is just a "he said, she said" misunderstanding. Sometimes the two adversaries realize they have been manipulated by another child, and they send for that person to help resolve the situation.

We are often asked if kids take advantage of this system to get out of a test or other schoolwork. Our answer is that teachers worth their salt can always tell when they're being conned. In that case, they can tell the students to go to the Peace Room during recess.

Providing a separate room is important because it seems to settle students down as soon as they walk in. But it doesn't always work miracles. Sometimes the children simply agree not to be disagreeable and to keep out of each other's hair.

> Dear Sr. Constance,
>
> I need to talk to you about a problem that happened yesterday in music and now it is getting too big and people are taking things too far. I think we need to go to the peace table.
>
> Sincerely,
>
> K.M. 18 8th grade

Dear Sister Constance

Yesterday I had a argument with
and I don't want it to last. It all began whe
made fun of me and she laughed.
I was mad at her because she ⟨crossed out⟩ was my
friend. I told her that it wasn't funny but
she laugh. We got in a argument and she said she
would get her aunt and I said I am getting going
to see my sister. ⟨crossed out⟩ Today we had to
help the second grade room. ⟨crossed out⟩ Some people came
up to me and told me that she was going
to fight me. I didn't want to fight so
I told I wrote this letter. Sister Constance
may I please she   at the peace table.

Sister Constance:

I offer to help if the Peace Room users want adult
support. But students usually don't want anyone in
the room except those directly involved. They tell us
that it takes a lot of work to make peace and that it's
easier to do when they're away from others.

When we ask why they don't want peer mediators,
they explain that sometimes they "give in"—they
don't really know the word compromise—and they
don't want others to know. Saving face is very important. There is so much violence where our children live; they have to exist on those mean streets.

One time an administrator from a tough pub-
lic-school district came to see the Peace Room. We
asked on the PA for any students who had used the
Peace Room that year and were willing to talk about
it. At least 40 kids from all grades came running
down the halls.

We were surprised at the number because we keep no records. The administrator asked the children about their experiences, and someone admitted, "It's not magic, or easy; sometimes we have to come back again."

Sister Jeannette:

We think it's important to help the children work through the process even if we're not in the room with them. I'll often ask, "Let me know what your peace plan is when you're finished."

One day I noticed that two girls who had entered the Peace Room full of anger had been in there for quite a long time. Quietly I checked to see what was going on. Both girls had their heads down, praying softly for a way to resolve their differences. I will always remember how they looked and how much better they got along afterwards.

It took quite a while for these two 8th grade girls to make peace, but both agreed that it was worth the effort.

Another time, a girl in my classroom and I were not getting along. Oh, how she got on my last nerve! (I'm sure the feeling was mutual.) I finally said to her, "We need to go to the Peace Room." What an experience that was for both of us. She told me I always noticed her first if I thought something was going on. I told her that I try very hard to be fair but felt she was constantly rolling her eyes when I gave the class instructions and that she was always at the center of whatever was not going well in the class. This brief time at the Peace Table made all the difference. I promised to give her the benefit of the doubt, and she promised to be careful about how she reacted to direction. The tension between us eased, and we peacefully coexisted throughout the remainder of the year.

NON-VIOLENCE TRAINING

We had outside organizations come to the school to provide non-violence training. Following each session the students were to write a summary of the lesson. One 8th grade girl turned in the following:

Today we talked about why people would or might fear death. One thing I never really thought about was naturally dying. I guess I hear so much about kids getting shot, or beat up, that it never occurred to me that somebody could actually die of having aids or cancer.

As a matter of fact, I can't even remember the last time I heard that somebody died without violence being committed.

THE PEACEMAKER ASSEMBLY: Year-End Culmination

The next step was creating the Peacemaker Assembly—an annual end-of-year much anticipated event to honor all the students on the Peace Wall and to award a Peacemaker medal to one older student and one younger student, our own sort of Nobel Peace Prize.

The medal quickly became a coveted prize, and the rituals surrounding the assembly the culmination of the school year. The medal is a gold-colored disc, three inches in diameter attached to a blue and gold ribbon—our school colors. One side depicts a pair of hands reaching out to shake; the other is engraved with St. Francis de Sales Peacemaker and the year of the award.

Because the auditorium cannot seat the whole student body, we hold the Peacemaker Assembly twice: once for K–3 students and once for 4–8 students. A blue banner stretches 30 feet above the stage with yellow letters spelling out St. Francis de Sales Peacemaker Assembly. A second banner, attached to the stage curtain, proclaims *A New Kind of Hero*.

Sister Jeannette:

> *The Peacemaker Assembly is the major event of the year—by far the biggest. I tell the eighth graders that their participation in the Peace Assembly is their final gift to the children who look up to them and will follow in their footsteps. "You are grownups teaching the little children now." And they take it seriously.*
>
> *The school has the national flag of every country that our students or their parents come from, and the assembly begins with a procession of these flags— almost 50 of them.*

After a greeting, about 20 second graders act out Isaiah 11:6, the Biblical lesson about the wolf dwelling with the lamb and the leopard lying down with the goat. Yes, the biblical message is the same, but we adapt to whatever stuffed animals the 8th graders have that year—maybe friendship between a moose and a giraffe, for instance.

'For a little child shall lead them...They will not hurt or destroy on all my holy mountain...' Isaiah 11 as portrayed by young children at the annual Peacemaker Assembly.

Next is the play. Sister Jeannette works with the graduating class to develop a fresh production every year but always with the same message: the importance of resolving differences peacefully. We take the storyline from myths, fables, and folk stories.

One year, for example, the eighth graders came out carrying large letters pasted on three-by-four-foot cardboard posters. The blue vowels were delicate looking, and the bearers made high-pitched sounds; the sturdy red consonants made deep, husky noises.

The vowels and consonants lined up on opposite sides and acted as if they were at war with one another, making threatening noises and miming rock-throwing. But then two courageous letters, W and Y—the two that can be either vowels or consonants—emerged from the battle and yelled, "STOP!"

Once they got the other letters' attention, W and Y explained that if they all cooperated, they could make wonderful words together. With that, the two sides stopped fighting and asked the audience to say the words that the two groups of letters formed together: PEACE, JOY, FRIEND, LOVE, PRAY, and more. Finally, all the letters joined in singing the ABC song as they skipped through the crowd and out of the auditorium. I doubt if many eighth graders would take this sort of thing on—at least not willingly. Yet our kids did, happy as can be. Street savvy eighth-grade boys danced down the aisle singing the ABCs—and they were joined by the whole audience!

Eighth-grade students display one of the positive words that a 'peaceful' Alphabet can form if the Consonants and Vowels would stop their fighting.

After the play, it is time to name all the children nominated as Peacemakers that year so they can stand and be recognized. We pick an eighth grader who is a good reader to call out the names. It takes practice for that person, since the children are from so many different countries and have names that are not at all familiar.

After we initiated the Peace Wall, several mothers said their children were discouraged because they were trying so hard to be peacemakers but never got noticed. We responded by putting up a plaque honoring the Unknown Peacemaker. At the Peace Assembly, Sister Constance tells the children who have not been publicly honored to close their eyes and consider whether they have worked for peace. She explains about the Tomb of the Unknown Soldier at Arlington Cemetery and says the Unknown Peacemaker plaque honors all students whose peacemaking has gone unrecognized.

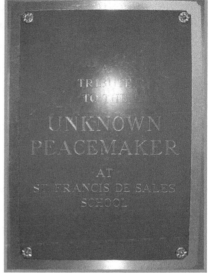

The Unknown Peacemaker Plaque

Sister Jeannette:

> *Next, dressed in graduation gowns, the eighth graders sing Mariah Carey's 1993 hit song "Hero." They really get into it as the little ones watch intently.*

The 8th grade class performs song and movement of 'Hero' at the Peacemaker Assembly

Finally, it's the moment everyone is waiting for—awarding of the Peace Medal.

The faculty meets beforehand to select a younger and an older medal winner from the students on the Peace Wall. We focus on children who had the courage to not fight and to not put others down by word or deed: someone who positively affected those around them. And then we take a vote.

The outcome is kept secret except that I call the parents of the two winners and invite them to attend the assembly without telling their child. Tears and exclamations of joy accompany the news to the parents every year. On assembly day, the parents wait unseen behind the stage curtains.

The announcement of the medal recipient is always greeted with cheering and a standing ovation. The parents come out from behind the stage, and there are usually lots of tears and often balloons and flowers. One recent year the younger medal recipient, a little third grade boy, was so stunned that he couldn't speak; he just stood frozen in place and stared.

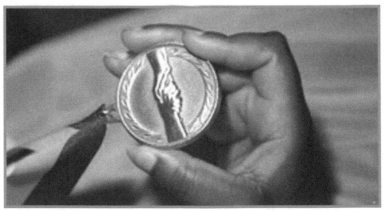

After we place the medal around the winner's neck and take pictures, the procession of flag bearers marches out and the assembly is over—though hopefully not really over but appropriated into each little heart.

Often we receive requests for "our peace curriculum," but we always answer that there is none. Being a peacemaker is a way of life at St. Francis de Sales.

How to Make a Peacemaker
(by a First Grader – uncorrected)

1 Step: To be Peacemaker you have to decide, for exzapoul, helping your friend.

2 Step: And get a bandayd for them! Be careful you can hurt them.

3 Step: And you can help an old ladey across the St. or the teacher.

4 Step: And when ther's a fight you can break it up!

5 Step: And when pepol don't sit proberly on the rug you can take care of that!

6 Step: And there you have it you are a Peasemaker!

TWO GRADUATES LOOK BACK:

Nguyet Tran '95 and John Supple '95

Nguyet Tran, 34, has a BA from Temple University and an MA from the University of Pennsylvania. Navy Lt. Commander John Supple, 34, is an Annapolis graduate currently pursuing an MBA from Georgetown (on hold while on assignment).

Nguyet and John, who met in kindergarten at St. Francis de Sales, are married and live with their two young children in Washington, D.C. Their siblings also attended St. Francis, and Nguyet's father was the janitor there for many years.

—

Our First Years at de Sales

Nguyet: *Although I was born in the United States, I was put in a kindergarten class with all Vietnamese children. The Vietnamese Christian Brother who taught was very strict, and I spent my first days at de Sales leaning out the window and sobbing. I tried to run away from school several times. Sister Constance saw how unhappy I was and switched my room.*

John: *I don't remember much from kindergarten, only that I was infatuated with Nguyet, and she barely tolerated me.*

In first grade, our desks were lined up in rows facing each other, and Nguyet sat right across from me. They used to sell pretzels in the morning at school. One day I'd forgotten my dime to buy a pretzel, and I sat and watched Nguyet eat her pretzel. I reached across to her desk and collected the salt that dropped off the pretzel with my finger. In retrospect, I wasn't really that hungry. I just wanted to get her attention! I knew even then that she was something.

Nguyet: *He was so annoying. I spent a lot of time tattling on him. He was always doing something.*

John: *I remember telling another girl, whom I had a crush on at the time, that there was someone else I thought I would marry. They gave out awards for the highest-grade average, one in each class. I won it in first grade, and every year after that her dad would ask her where I ranked in the class.*

Nguyet: *John was the only white kid in the class.*

John: *I don't remember that. I think there were others, weren't there?*

Nguyet: *Race was never an issue at St. Francis de Sales. I was aware of the differences that existed in the neighborhood. I was very independent when I was little and walked to school with my little brother.*

I was born in Philly to parents who escaped from Vietnam, a topic I only learned about when Sister Jeannette asked me if my parents came from North or South Vietnam. At that time, I had no idea. Sister Jeannette insisted that I find out about their flight from Vietnam to the United States and learn all that I could about my heritage. I learned the story of how they left Vietnam the day the Communists took over in 1975. I will always be grateful to her that I learned about it.

A Changing Relationship

John: *The only difference between Vietnamese Catholics and Irish Catholics is that one eats a lot of rice and the other eats a lot of potatoes! That's it. They both have huge families. I am the oldest of five kids and Nguyet is the seventh of eight siblings. Both take their religion very seriously, though they like to have a good time.*

Our relationship began to change in 8th grade when we were both selected for a special math program at West Catholic High School, 12 blocks away. We would walk from SFDS to the program together with a third friend, Rahat, a Bengali classmate who remains a close friend to this day. Nguyet and I started dating in our junior year.

Nguyet: *My dad didn't like the idea that I was dating a white boy. He used to leave the house as soon as John came over. I think it was really that my dad didn't want me dating at all. We maintained a long-distance relationship while John was at the Naval Academy and I was attending Temple, later earning an MA in education from University of Pennsylvania.*

John: *We knew we wanted to get married. We were done with the long-distance thing. We had a small courthouse wedding in 2004 in Corpus Christi and then were married again at St. Francis de Sales Parish Church in 2005 with a big party.*

Nguyet: *We had a formal Vietnamese engagement. His family presented my family with a roasted pig!*

John: *My family loved this. The pig had to be covered in red cellophane because red is the symbol of joy.*

Back to St. Francis de Sales

Nguyet: *Everyone looked forward to getting older so we could start practicing for the speech competition. We practiced constantly with a partner coach. I was very shy, and in the final competition didn't do very well, but I competed. It was a personal victory!*

John: *Sister Jeannette wasn't just interested in those who had the highest grade-point average. In eighth grade, she got all 30 kids to work on a speech.*

Nguyet: *We didn't realize it at the time, but as an adult and now an educator, I know how important it is to get students to come out of their shells and work together. I would have never done the speech competition on my own, but working together with other kids made me want to do well. We needed our peers to critique us to get better. As I've grown up, I've learned how much we can gain from the critiques of others. We started developing those skills early on.*

John: *I learned some sayings from Sister Jeannette that I continue to use today. "Can't means won't," for example. Sister Jeannette also used to say that tests are not something to dread but something to look forward to, to show how smart and well prepared you are, "an opportunity to excel." That stuck with me over the years. I'm a big advocate of testing and high standards. I still can recite the square roots that Sister Jeannette taught us, up to 225. At one point, we knew all the way up to 30 squared!*

Nguyet: Everyone wanted to be nominated as a Peacemaker. It was a big deal. You got your picture on the Peace Wall. It wasn't just about not fighting; it was about making the right choices and walking away from bad situations.

John: There were many students at de Sales with difficult lives, but the Sisters never accepted excuses. They were compassionate and gave us the sense that "we're giving you opportunities, don't make excuses."

How would I describe St. Francis de Sales? Challenging, welcoming, Catholic with a big "C" and a little "c."

Nguyet: Always diverse, and fun, that's what I remember. Perhaps the biggest lesson we learned: Don't hold back. There's nothing to be afraid of.

CHAPTER SIX

A Refugee and an American

Two Graduates' Stories:

The following stories of Futsum, a refugee, and Josh, an American child, make us realize that those years were something special, and despite the peaks and valleys, it was all worthwhile! We feel these two young men undoubtedly represent many others like them who passed through our school during our 31 years at St. Francis de Sales.

We cannot be grateful enough to all of them for what they shared with us, taught us, and demanded by their very beings. We are honored by this privilege and acknowledge that we have been blessed.

A GRADUATE LOOKS BACK:

Futsum Merhazion '87

Futsum Merhazion, 42, resides in Alexandria, Virginia, where he works as an IT auditor, with a title of Senior Business Systems Analyst, for a government contractor. Futsum was one of the first Eritrean refugees at SFDS. He married an Ethiopian woman, and their first child was born in July 2014. A graduate of West Catholic High School in Philadelphia, Futsum earned a partial scholarship to the University of Pittsburgh where he majored in economics with a minor in statistics. He has an MBA from Georgetown. Of Futsum's eight siblings, two of his younger brothers and his younger sister also attended SFDS. He identifies himself as a Catholic and, "without a question," would send his children to SFDS.

—

After escaping from Eritrea, my family had been sponsored by an agency that helped us move into an apartment in North Philly. I'd attended 6th and 7th grade there, mostly taking ESOL classes. Then we met a mutual friend of the Sisters who thought we would be better off at St. Francis de Sales.

We moved to West Philly, and I started de Sales in 8th grade, later repeating the grade because my English was so poor. I needed a lot of hand-holding, and Sister Jeannette was there. She was very involved with helping me, and I was lucky enough to have her for two years! She is an unforgettable individual.

I was constantly bothering Sister J. I needed someone to talk to and remember sitting with her many days after school, talking, just talking. Sister J was willing to listen. It helped me. I had a lot of things to say and didn't know how to say them. She listened.

I don't know how it happened, but I accidently wrote a poem. When Sister J discovered that I'd written it, she urged me to write more. She encouraged me and edited my work. Some of my poems were published in a magazine for young people! I would have never thought of doing things like that. I didn't feel what I was doing was that important, but she thought highly of it.

I spoke to her about how the Ethiopian-Eritrean War affected my life and how no one could truly understand. Somehow, Sister J seemed to know what I felt, maybe because she'd had a lot of experience with Vietnamese and kids from other war-torn countries before me. There was nothing I felt I could not talk to her about.

Instead of going home and watching TV, I was actively engaged in writing poetry. It kept my mind occupied...the right way. I haven't written recently but I'd like to get back to it.

For so long, Sister Constance and Sister Jeannette and SFDS have been educating kids who are new to America. They have amazing experience dealing with students from terrible war zone areas of the world.

Sister Jeannette remembers:

My first memory of Futsum was seeing him sit rather glumly in the second desk in the third row just watching, taking it all in. This was his persona for a long time, as he seemed reluctant to engage. Every once in a while, there was a statement or comment that made me realize that much was going on inside that young man.

Once during an Earth Science lesson, I made the statement that deserts are beautiful, recalling my visit to Death Valley and Joshua Tree National Park. From that third-row desk I heard, "Not if you have to escape across one!" Ensuing discussions related the horrors Futsum's family encountered during their 23-day escape across the Sahara, a far cry from my experience in Death Valley! The poem he penned about his last day in Eritrea is heartrending:

ERITREAN FAREWELL

The night passed
The day came
The sun shone
The plants wakened
The birds sang.

The sun changed the ground into fire
It was too sunny
for the plants to dance
and the birds to sing.

I looked straight at the sun.
Water dropped from my eyes

It was time to leave
It was our secret.

Silently my mouth said 'Goodbye . . .'
But my heart was not ready

There were so many other lessons I learned from Futsum over the course of those two years he spent in 8th grade and then as a high school and college student. What a proud day it was when, as college students, he and Choun took me to lunch at a small restaurant in Old City Philadelphia! They had come so far, accomplished so much . . .

So who, to me, is Futsum? Futsum represents the hundreds of children, both immigrants and refugees, who passed through our doors with their stories: their knowledge of the politics and love for their native countries, their struggles learning English (so strange to many of them without knowledge of A B C characters), their wonder at all that the United States embodies, their love of learning and determination to study, their memories, the horrors they lived through, their willingness to get up each day and go on, and the GIFT they are to our United States of America.

CHAPTER 6

A Graduate Looks Back:

Joshua Walls '07

Josh Walls, 22, the first in his immediate family to attend college, is a 2015 graduate of Syracuse University in sports management. During college, he landed coveted internships at ESPN, Creative Artists Agency, IMG Management Group, and Syracuse's minor league hockey and baseball teams, but when interviewed during spring of his senior year, he was "still not 100% sure which way to go after graduation." A few of his cousins went to SFDS— one is an investment banker with Merrill Lynch, another an entertainment attorney, while a third not only graduated from SFDS, but also became a teacher there.

—

I transferred to SFDS in 2nd grade. It wasn't a big transition for me; I was young and didn't really know anything different. SFDS is very much a family atmosphere. I've known two of my three current best friends since second or third grade at SFDS.

I come from a single parent household. My mom raised me and we lived with my grandmother. Mom went back to school while I was at de Sales. I'm very proud of her. She became an LPN, things got better, and we were able to move out of Grand's. I still have great relationships with my mom and my grandma.

I remember my first encounter with Sister Jeannette. I got into trouble. It was in fourth grade, and I and a couple of other kids were making noise while leaving the building at dismissal time. Sister J caught us and made us sit in her classroom while she graded papers. I remember it as if it were yesterday. Everyone said Sister J was scary—she's missing a finger, you know—but when I was able to have her as a teacher, I learned she was one of the sweetest people in the world. She was definitely one of the greatest teachers I've ever had.

We learned diversity on so many levels at SFDS—to be accepting of people from other races, countries, and cultures. My best friend from de Sales is Eritrean, and there is no difference between us. De Sales helped us all to understand that people are people at the end of the day.

I used to get in trouble at first. They were so serious about the smallest things, like talking in class. But sometimes, small things can become larger things. Talking in class when you're not supposed to ultimately shows a lack of discipline. As I became older, I learned to appreciate such things. By the time I got to Sister Jeannette's class, I was on the straight and narrow. Prior to her, I was lucky to have Sister Constance and several of my other SFDS teachers in my life.

While in high school, I was the youngest person to write for the Philadelphia Inquirer, and I participated in a debate program where we were coached by attorneys from Stradley Ronon, one of Philadelphia's top litigation firms. I chose Syracuse University and majored in sports management after someone at church told me, "It doesn't matter what you major in, just do something you really want to do." College was special. I worked hard and was president of every organization I joined. I am very thankful that I had the great opportunity of going to college. I just loved it.

I am a firm believer that no one makes it alone, and I think a lot about the impact of SFDS on my life. Things absolutely would have been different for me without it. I appreciate SFDS, knowing that other kids in my situation didn't have such an opportunity. I did a lot of growing there!

Sister Constance reflects:

Yes, Joshua "did a lot of growing up" at de Sales. By the time Joshua reached sixth grade, I had a pile of poor conduct reports about him from music, gym and art teachers, as well as from every classroom teacher. It was time for a showdown with Joshua. His mother had been asked to come for conferences many times during the previous three years. I took him to the Peace Room and showed him all of the reports, telling him he would have to change if he wanted to stay at de Sales. He seemed surprised by the reports, had not realized there were so many, nor that he had been building a case file against himself. During this heart-to-heart (firm, but kind) talk that day, Joshua promised me that he would turn his life around . . . and he did! There was never another negative report about Josh for his remaining years. Not only that, he became an outstanding student and a fine man of character. He makes us proud!

Futsum and Josh represent the strength that can be realized with the integration of the new arrivals from foreign lands with American-born children, the ones who assisted the young refugees and immigrants in adjusting to life in an unfamiliar country. We need more 'WELCOME' Schools, not WALLS in America!

CHAPTER SEVEN

Daily Ups and Downs

As we review those early years at de Sales, we thought we'd like to end with a potpourri of some memorable days and quotes that give glimpses of daily life at our school. It was indeed a rollercoaster ride of joys and sorrows!

A TRAUMATIC DAY

Tamika, a little third grader, burst through the door, ran down the hallway, and threw her arms around Sister Constance. She was sobbing uncontrollably, and it took several minutes of soothing words to find out what had happened to her. Finally, she was able to say that when she went into the corner store on the way to school to buy chips, a man came into the store and shot the owner. Sister Constance continued to hold her close and assure her that she was safe now at school. When she finally gained control, she looked up with tear-filled eyes and said, "But you don't understand. That's the <u>second</u> time this happened to me!"

COWS AND GOATS IN WEST PHILLY?

An intriguing advertisement came in the mail and we jumped right on it. A farmer would spread hay in our school yard and bring farm animals for the children to enjoy. Well...our kids were scared to death. They wanted no part of touching a cow, or a pig, or a chicken, or...Especially surprising was the reaction of the eighth graders who were asked to pal with a first grader to help them learn about the animals. No way!! They're tough in some ways but not others.

ROUTINE...A REALITY CHECK

Sister Jeannette received an absence note: Dear Sis, please excuse Susan for not coming to school yesterday. She was sick from taking a whole bottle of pills. Thank you.

Taron's mother called to ask how much it would cost to buy a new set of textbooks for her son. Upon questioning, she said that her son had been attacked, beaten, and robbed of his backpack on the way home from school. One more act of violence in the neighborhood. For us, the cost of books was not an issue. They could be given to Taron. We had already tried to set up safe passage procedures after an 8th grader had two teeth knocked out on his way home from school. Our concern was always <u>how to keep our children safe</u>?

UNEDITED:

As soon as incoming students had enough basic skills with English, Sister Jeannette asked them to write about their homeland and tell how they arrived in the USA. Today, she has a treasure trove of primary source stories in their own words.

Kate: "How is live in Poland: The time is very hard in Poland. The people can buy only meet on 'stamps food' and like fruit and vegetable are not there." Farther along in her story she wrote, "There are difference between United States and Poland. The difference are, you cannot buy gun and shoot someone so easy as in United States."

DANCING WITH THE STARS

Yes, our fifth graders became the stars of the school and the city when we received a grant to provide the entire class with ballroom dancing lessons. The popularity of the TV show made the project an instant hit with the kids, and we loved watching them. They went on to win the gold medal in district competition and took the silver medal in the city finals at the Merriam Theatre in Center City.

MEMORABLE ONE-LINERS

A second grader: "My teacher told us to save for a rainy day. I guess to buy an umbrella!"

An immigrant parent about a new first grader with no lunch, "Oh, no, she doesn't need food during the day! She never had it in our country."

A kindergartner was overheard talking about two Caucasian teachers: "They're not white. If they were white, they would have told us!"

A third grader about a new immigrant: "Don't worry, Sister Constance. We'll take good care of her."

A nine-year-old visitor who stopped by with his mother: "Mom, why doesn't my school feel like this?

A fourth-grade girl: "Do you have to have blue eyes to be a nun?" (We had not realized that in a school with just about all African American, African, Asian, and Hispanic children, WE were the only ones with BLUE EYES!)

Ngoc, a newly arrived refugee, said in complete seriousness, "I'm afraid to go outside to play because they told me it rains cats and dogs in America."

Claire, a third-grade American girl: "My best friends are twins. Duong is from Vietnam, and Chien is from China."

In conversation with a second-grade girl from Africa, Sister Constance was told that she wouldn't have to be afraid to visit the child's country because "even though we have many snakes, they do not bite pregnant women." She thought Sister Constance was the MOTHER, not just the PRINCIPAL!

TRACK EVENTS

Our newly formed track team practices each day in the spring by running around the block and jumping over cracked sidewalks, broken tree trunks, trashcans, fire hydrants, and any cars that may have been parked on the sidewalk. To our surprise, they won medals in the first couple of meets in which they participated, and then for two years in a row, they won the gold medal for the 4 x 100 at the famous Penn Relays! After that, one young athlete explained, "Do you see, when we get on a <u>REAL</u> track, we can really run!" Those bronze plaques are lovingly caressed by visitors young and old.

One day a volunteer was working after school when she heard loud screaming. She looked out the window, saw a strange man yelling, and our children running away. Immediately, she dialed 911. The police arrived only to discover that the track coach was just trying to get the team to run faster. Our track coach father happened to be an off-duty cop himself, so we resolved that incident without letting him get arrested. The officers had a good laugh!

THE CONSTITUTION

In 1987, we were celebrating the 200th anniversary of the Constitution. Sister Jeannette dedicated a social studies lesson to this historic event and then asked the class to enter a contest about the Constitution using art or poetry or an essay, as directed by the guidelines. The students eagerly engaged in the project and in all earnestness, Amira asked for some advice. Sister leaned over the desk to examine the poem that was in its first draft and Amira asked, "How many people were at that meeting for the Constitution? I can't remember whether it was our four (fore) fathers or our five fathers."

THIS SCHOOL HAS AIDS

The Little School is located across the street and houses our two kindergartens and two first grades. It creates a homey atmosphere for the little ones as they begin their education, but the drawback was that there was no office there and the doors were all locked for safety reasons. Therefore, the doorbell would ring with parents bringing late children, forgotten lunches, etc. The rejoicing of the teachers could not be measured when the wonderful Hamilton Foundation provided salaries for teacher aides. However, the note that a teacher tacked onto the front door caused some concern. "Please don't knock on the door. Take your children and lunches to the main office in the Big School and they will be taken care of there. This school has AIDS." The elimination of the all-important 'e' had to be corrected immediately!

WHAT'S IN A NAME?

Fai Sin came from China, and his family quickly realized that his last name might cause difficulty. They just changed the last letter of his name. He is on our list of graduates as Fai Sim, and he visits every few years (to have us meet his growing family) and is doing very well.

We had several Vietnamese children named Dung who went

through our school, and there was never any problem with the name because our city children did not know the word "dung."

It all changed when a new boy came from Mongolia and his name was pronounced Ah-shit. Oh, the bedlam that ensued! Everyone wanted to talk to him and call him by name, including the teachers. Soon he came to realize the situation and began to say, "Oh, just call me Archie." And Archie he became. However, for those who knew, it was a password, and whenever some of us were really upset about something and felt like cursing, we would call out "Archie" and everybody knew what we meant!

WE ARE ONE FAMILY

On another day, a Buddhist father rang the convent doorbell and announced, "In refugee camp they tell us, 'When you get to America, look for a Catholic School.'" And we took his children. It turned out that the father knew he was dying and wanted his family settled in America before he died... Several months later, his burial service took place in a funeral parlor in South Philly and we attended. A Buddhist monk, robed in orange, arrived from D.C. Incense was burning in front of the coffin, the photos to honor the deceased were set up on small tables, and behind the coffin lit by the morning sun were two stained glass windows, one of the Sacred Heart and one of the Blessed Mother. The God of us all was present that day!

LISTEN AND LEARN

One day an American eighth grade boy acted up in the classroom and publicly 'dissed' the new teacher. When Sister Constance heard about it, she took the boy and stood him in front of the class to publicly apologize for the disrespect he had shown. For her, the matter was over, but after school some of the boys were in the classroom as she passed by and waved to them. "Sister, come here. Today you scared the other kids, but you didn't scare us, 'CAUSE WE KNOW WORSER THINGS!" They then began to describe the punishments by teachers in their countries: kneeling on cracked seashells on the beach with arms extended and a huge rock in each hand, beatings with bamboo, karate kicks, etc., and they concluded, "That's why you didn't scare us."

WHO'S IN CHARGE?

During the summer after the arrival of our Laotian and Hmong children, we heard that one of our seventh-grade girls was married the day after school closed for the summer. The girl had a disagreement with her father and ran to stay overnight with the family of her boyfriend. When the elders of the community received word that she had stayed in her boyfriend's home, they ordered a marriage to take place. This was despite the fact that the boyfriend's parents and family were present and said that it was all right with them. With that event we learned that the elders of a village had more power than the parents in a family, and they had to be obeyed.

DAMAGE CONTROL

We were always advised that the best way to handle the media after a problem is to speak as honestly and openly as possible without revealing professional information. I was ready to act on this advice when a young boy who was in our school in seventh grade transferred out with no reason. A few weeks into the new year, he stopped by to tell us how great his new school was. Several days later, he shot himself to death in his bedroom in the presence of a friend who was a student at de Sales and his own six-year-old brother. I waited expectantly for the media. We grieved as a school, some of us attended his funeral, and NO ONE ever came near us, nor did anything ever appear on TV or in the newspaper. I had not relished the idea of speaking publicly, but I experienced a deep sorrow that this young life was gone, and nobody had noticed.

WHERE THERE'S A WILL...

Vannda did not yet speak English, but she managed to communicate that she wanted to be in the show 'Peter Pan' when she saw children go to practice every day after school. This was a challenge for a new refugee, and we explained it to the director of the show. No one was smiling more than Vannda when she was assigned the role of Tinkerbell. Without uttering a word, she fluttered her fairy wings across the stage and shone as a star in the performance!

SHOOTING, DANCING, RUNNING

Aman was six years old when he arrived from a refugee camp in Kenya along with nine brothers and sisters. His older sister later told us that he was special because he had a great skill with a sling shot and had killed enough birds to keep the family alive! (A biblical David among us!) Some years later, this same lad was on the team that brought us the Ballroom Dancing Finals silver cup. His talents continued to blossom when a year after that, he was on the relay team that won first place in the Penn Relays! Does Magic Happen at de Sales for children, or what!!

St. John ended his Gospel with these words: There were also many other things that Jesus did; if all were written down, the world itself, I suppose, would not hold all the books that would have to be written (John 21:25).

And so it is with us—there are many more years, children, and stories that would not fit in this book. They will have to come later!

Epilogue

Lessons, Reflections, and Thanks

+

J.M.J.A.T.

Villa Maria House of Studies
Immaculata, Pennsylvania 19345

Dear Sister Mary Jeannette Lucey,

      You are appointed by Holy Obedience

to: Saint Matthew, Philadelphia

for: Assist in Development

      May God bless your obedience, dear Sister.

      Devotedly in Mary's Immaculate Heart,

      Sister Lorraine McGrew, IHM

Tuesday, 7th Week of Easter
Date: May 19, 2015

And so it happened—the two of us were a part of St. Francis de Sales for 31 years—the first 25 as principal and 8th grade teacher, the last six as Co-directors of Development. In 2015, we said an emotional goodbye and headed to a new assignment at St. Matthew Parish in Northeast Philadelphia, where we are now Development Directors for the school there.

Looking back at our three decades at St. Francis de Sales School, we see much change—positive change, we believe. The surrounding neighborhood is also far different from the one we found in 1984, though there the change may not be beneficial for everyone; with gentrification now on the march, most families that send children to the school today cannot afford to live nearby.

Along with the changes, we see in those 31 years many lessons. In this little book, we have tried to distill and give context to that learning. Here are five key lessons from our St. Francis experience that we believe may be of value to others who work with and care about children:

> 1. There are always going to be bumps in the road; naming them challenges rather than problems makes all the difference. Recognizing challenges is not the same as admitting defeat.

> 2. Children need to tell their stories; make sure to listen to them. Treasured memories of homeland and family live in the hearts of immigrants despite the horrific conditions they may have left behind. All children have stories.

> 3. Diversity is a challenge but also an opportunity. Remember that culture and community are two different things. It is possible to create one community out of many cultures.

> 4. There is potential and promise in all children. Children can do anything when you believe in them, encourage them, provide them with a safe place to do whatever their thing is—AND CELEBRATE EVERYTHING.

> 5. Children want and need to be given a practical alternative to fighting. By celebrating good and peaceful behavior, it is possible to eliminate almost all physical fighting. The Peace Room was an answer for us!

Sister Constance:

> *Thirty-one years in one mission is unusual in religious life, but, then, nothing about life at St. Francis de Sales is usual.*

> *The focus of all those years was the children: their beautiful faces, their hopes, their dreams, and our dreams for them. Although many days were extremely difficult, the rewards far surpassed the challenges.*

> *Most of the stories we recount in this book come from our early years at de Sales; there are many more we could tell. But we hope that the few here are enough to encourage readers to listen to children and believe in them, and to welcome and educate immigrants and refugees.*

> *Our purpose is to spread the word that every effort possible should be made to unfold the potential in a budding child so that he or she can become a beautiful flower to enhance this world and the next.*

Sister Jeannette:

> *After years of telling our stories, actually putting them down on paper brought about a whole rush of memories and sentiments: smiles, laughter, and pride but also sadness and tears.*

> *Much to my surprise, what forced itself to the surface above all was the SHOULDS. For many, if not most, of my years at St. Francis, I was tortured with "I should do this. I need to do that." The many hours of the workday, often stretching into the night,*

brought exhaustion, pain—and guilt. There were so many kids, so many issues, so many needs, so many projects—so many SHOULDS—that it could be overwhelming. I simply couldn't do all that I felt needed doing.

It seems funny that these stories should bring back those feelings. I always insisted that my students look people in the eye. Perhaps now is the time to look <u>my</u> SHOULDS in the eye and see that what transpired was the best for <u>that</u> time and for <u>those</u> kids—to see that being part of their lives and doing what was doable counted.

What I know is that by defying stereotypes of race, sex, ethnicity, and culture, we wheedled from these young vessels full of promise and possibility some <u>thing</u> wonderful, some <u>one</u> wonderful!

A LITANY OF THANKS

We conclude with our thanks and appreciation to so many.

First to:

- The parents who chose to send children to St. Francis de Sales

- The teachers and staff who shared our journey

- The hundreds of St. Francis de Sales students who taught us so much about life

- The benefactors and graduates who supported our mission

We also thank you, the reader, for taking time to enter our world. We hope and pray that you will be inspired to do one or more of the following:

- Become a teacher

- Teach your own children to accept all types of people

- Reach out to immigrants and refugees

- Realize that all children—rich, poor, and in-between— deserve an excellent education

- Believe that children can do anything, if <u>you</u> believe in <u>them</u>

- Support our new ministry at St. Matthew School ~ 3040 Cottman Avenue ~ Philadelphia PA 19149 ~ Attention: Sr. Jeannette Lucey.

OR . . . . .BECOME A NUN! It's a great and rewarding life!

CPSIA information can be obtained
at www.ICGtesting.com
Printed in the USA
BVHW051315101118
532611BV00002B/2/P